# Dating

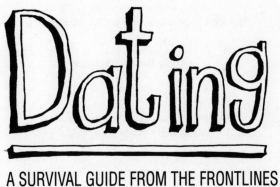

# Dating

## A SURVIVAL GUIDE FROM THE FRONTLINES

## JOSEY VOGELS

ADAMS MEDIA CORPORATION
Holbrook, Massachusetts

First published in the U.S. by Adams Media Corporation
260 Center Street, Holbrook, MA 02343.
This edition produced by arrangement with Raincoast Books.

ISBN: 1-58062-176-7

Printed in the United States of America.
J I H G F E D C B A

Library of Congress Cataloging in Publication Data
Available upon request from the publisher.

*Raincoast Books gratefully acknowledges the support of the Government of Canada, through the
Book Publishing Industry Development Program, the Canada Council for the Arts and the
Department of Canadian Heritage. We also acknowledge the assistance of the Province of British
Columbia, through the British Columbia Arts Council.*

Every effort was made to obtain permission to reproduce
copyrighted material excerpted in this book.

Excerpts from Beth L. Bailey's
From Front Porch to Back Seat: Courtship in Twentieth-Century America
reprinted by permission of Johns Hopkins University Press.
Book design by Raincoast Books.

*This book is available at quantity discounts for bulk purchases.
For information, call 1-800-872-5627.*

Visit our home page at http://www.adamsmedia.com

*To Chris, the best date I've ever had*

# Contents

# Acknowledgments

Thanks to all the folks at Raincoast Books for their belief in me. Thanks especially to Rachelle, my editor extraordinaire, for all her wonderful suggestions and her patience. Thanks to Denise, my agent, who helped make this book possible. Many thanks to my family and friends for their love and support and their bad dating stories. And oodles of thanks to all the wonderful people (you know who you are) who so graciously shared their insights and experiences. This book would not have been possible without you, and I owe you all a drink (or six). Finally, I couldn't have done this without my 3 P.M. date with Rosie to look forward to everyday.

# Welcome Troops

## A Word from the Frontlines

"I've had it with men!" "I don't understand women!" "What do women want?" "Why can't I meet someone?" "I don't know how to date!" "Why does it have to be so complicated?"

Welcome to dating in the age of the jaded.

Store bookshelves are loaded with books on how to salvage your relationship, save your marriage or hang on for dear life even when the whole thing is going to pot. The problem with all of these books is that they assume you have a relationship to hang onto in the first place.

From what I can tell, plenty of us can't even get that part together. Women are frustrated with men, men are confused about women, divorce rates are through the roof. So why do we even bother?

Because, despite all the frustration and confusion, deep down, no one really wants to go it alone. And let's face it, it'd be nice to have someone to feed the pigeons with when the eyesight starts to go. Unfortunately, this means we will continue in what sometimes seems like our futile struggle to meet "the one."

And, I hate to say it, but that means we have to date, or whatever we call it these days. Because who really "dates" anymore? At least we don't call it dating. Instead we say, "Would you like to get together sometime?" What, to discuss stock prices? Or, more likely, we meet someone in a bar, sleep with them, then decide if we want to "date."

In the old days, a date was a date. He was supposed to call you by Wednesday to ask you out for the following Saturday. The intention was clear. But most of us can't even plan what we're going to have for lunch each day, much less a date several days in advance. What if we change our minds by then?

Plus we're terrified of stating our intentions. Call it a date and suddenly it's laden with significance and, God forbid, expectations.

Hey, no one said it was going to be easy. In fact, it has to be a little difficult. If it was easy, we'd probably quickly grow bored with the whole mating game. And that wouldn't be much good for the species, now would it?

Still, we hate that we have to work at it. It makes us feel like losers to admit we need some help meeting people and dating. "It's supposed to happen naturally," we moan. The truth is, if you want to do anything well, you've got to work at it. Same with dating. You can settle for any old relationship or you can spend some time figuring out what you want and finding it. And that's not always so easy to do. Sometimes you need help.

Things were probably a little easier before we let our hearts have so much say in the matter. In fact, back in ancient Greek times, love was considered an amusing pastime at best, a distraction at worst. It certainly wasn't expected to change your life. And it wasn't something people necessarily looked for in a relationship. Back then marriage was more of a practical arrangement than a union of two people in love.

These days, our search for a mate with whom we can enjoy mad, passionate love – as well as compatibility, security and equality – has us looking for love in all the right places, the wrong places and every nook and cranny in between. And the harder we search for it, the more it hides, the more desperate we become and the more help we need to find it.

And, it seems, everywhere you turn, someone or something reminds you of your complete and utter failure as a human being because you are obviously incapable of accomplishing the one – apparently the ultimate – thing that justifies your existence here on Earth. You have failed to pair up.

At the same time, we're supposed to learn to enjoy being single, learn not to dwell on our loneliness, all the while remaining open and ready to meet people at all times.

I'm exhausted just writing about it.

With all this in mind, I headed out to the dating battlefield to find out what was going on. Most of the advice in this book is geared toward straight single folks in their 20s and 30s (sorry, but there are just more of them), and most of the people I talked to were, you guessed it, straight single folks in their 20s and 30s. But I interviewed all kinds of people in the dating trenches: gay and lesbian, divorced, older and younger people. Their experiences are reflected here as well.

I also turned to the readers of *My Messy Bedroom,* my syndicated sex-and-relationships column. I asked them to answer my questions about dating, and responses came from across Canada. People gave me the goods on everything from why it's so hard and what we are looking for to what we should wear on a first date. In addition, I consulted the dating experts, the matchmakers, the scientists and the history books.

The result is a humorous and (hopefully) helpful look at dating (or whatever the hell we call it these days), filled with the thoughts and personal stories of the people on the frontlines. Plus, you'll find plenty of tips and advice – and a few words of wisdom from my own trip around the dating block.

But before we get to all that, let me bring you up to date on the world of dating.

## Who Invented This System Anyway?

I guess you could call it my first "date."

It was 1977. I was 13. It was lunch hour on a rainy day and we were stuck inside our portable classroom. (We'd outgrown our tiny two-classroom Catholic schoolhouse.) We were doing the requisite horsing around and suddenly a bunch of our friends pushed me and Stephen Lewis out onto the wooden steps of the portable. There we were, standing in the rain, when Stephen looked at me and sputtered, "Will you go with me?" Staring at the ground, but without skipping a beat, I blurted, "Yes." Then we scrambled over each other as fast as we could back into the safety of the portable.

Call it unromantic, but that was our first date. Not even so much as a peck on the cheek at the end. And now we were officially "going together." I can't recall us ever actually going anywhere together, mind you. We did stand together in the yard once in a while. Eventually, another girl with slightly more to offer (they were huge for a 13-year-old) caught his fancy, and I was dropped like a hot potato.

In some ways, my experience with Stephen wasn't so different from the way my aunt got a date as a young woman back in Holland before World War II. She and her family lived out in the country, and every so often a group of young eligible bachelors would come calling on their bicycles. They'd all sit around and exchange niceties until bachelor No. 1 got the thumbs up from chosen girl. This was the cue for the others to take off, thus transforming the visit into an official date.

From the moment the first caveman dragged his woman off by the hair, we've had some strange ways of pairing off. It wasn't exactly called dating in prehistoric times, but it was just as unsavory as some of the things we go through today to find a match.

Later on, in ancient Greece, dad would hire a matchmaker to find a good husband and provider for his daughter. Love wasn't a big concern. Women hardly knew what love was, since they barely left the house. And hubby didn't care much if he loved her either. The missus was pretty much a baby-maker. He got his yas-yas elsewhere.

The whole concept of romantic love didn't really get off the ground until the

12th century, when the troubadours belted out the first love songs, and women were at least let out of the house. No one really knows why courtly love, as they called it back then, suddenly became so popular. Some say love was there all along, and people in the 12th century just named it and nurtured it. I figure it was a bit like potato chips: once you try one, you keep going back for more.

Dating as we know it didn't really catch on in the Western World until the 1920s. Even then, it didn't have such romantic beginnings. In the early 1900s, a "courtship" was usually arranged. If a young woman saw a hunky guy at church, let's say, her parents would decide if Mr. Hunky would be allowed to "call" on her. In another scenario, mom and dad would find some respectable and eligible young guy and invite him to "visit" their daughter in their parlor while they stood guard in the next room.

There were lots of rules. Only boys who were old enough to work and could support a wife were allowed to call. Parents decided how long the visit would last. If dad established after a couple of visits that the guy intended to marry the girl, he was to court the girl properly – you know, like invite her to a church social or a school picnic, always supervised, of course. If the couple did anything on their own, the folks had to know exactly where they were going and when they would be back.

Even then, the matchmaking parents were more concerned about whether the guy could provide their darling daughter with financial security than whether their daughter actually liked the guy or not.

It was the lower classes that really got the "dating" ball rolling. Even though they tried to emulate the "courtship" practices of the snooty, there were usually no "parlors" in the homes of the working class. Privacy was a bit of an issue. So they went out.

In fact, the first recorded uses of the word "date" in its modern meaning come from working-class slang. According to Beth L. Bailey's book, *From Front Porch to Back Seat* (1988), George Ade, a Chicago writer back in the 1890s, wrote a column for the *Chicago Record* about working-class life called "Stories of the Streets and the Town." In an issue of his column published in 1896, Ade told the tale of "Artie," a young man who asks his unfaithful girlfriend, "I s'pose the other boy's fillin' all my *dates*?" And in 1899, Bailey writes, Ade suggested that the power of a girl's charms could be measured by the fact that "her *Date* Book had to be kept on the Double Entry System."

By the beginning of the 20th century, the term "dating" was pretty much part of our vocabulary. Then, after World War I, the "Roaring Twenties" defined it even further.

During that war, soldiers were exposed to city life in Europe. Industrialization was kicking in, and coming back home to life on the farm didn't quite cut it. Everyone started moving to the city where life was more expensive, and mom needed to work too. Dad was no longer the sole breadwinner. Women also got the vote and became equal citizens with men, at least on paper.

Then the advent of the telephone meant you could call someone up for a "date," and the popularization of cars and movie theaters meant there were places you could take someone out to. Booze loosened things up even more. By the mid-twenties, "dating," as we know it, was firmly in place.

It took a while before this new form of "dating" gained respect, however. Young people loved it, but their parents weren't so crazy about it. They had a hard time accepting that their kids could make plans to meet and spend time together unsupervised, with no specific commitment in mind. But, slowly, the older generation caved in, and it didn't take long for young people to make their own rules about dating.

Not that society still didn't have a say. In fact, it wasn't long before etiquette books, advice books and women's magazines started to give their opinions about dating. Eventually, everyone was getting the same tips about dating, despite class or background.

Advertising got on board with the birth of slogans like, "Say It with Flowers" and "'Til Breath Do Us Part." Because, of course, you couldn't hitch a man unless you did something about your bad breath.

Not surprisingly, as a fairly new social phenomenon, the concept of dating was quickly open for analysis. Margaret Mead was one of the first social scientists to critique the whole notion of dating as it developed. As early as 1920, Mead said that even this new form of dating was not about love or courtship or finding a marriage partner. Rather, she said it was more like a contest to give young people a feeling of success and popularity. It forced girls to be competitive, and it was actually detrimental to marriage because it taught women to act coy and fend off boys, which was lousy training for becoming an equal partner.

Later, in 1937, Willard Waller, another social scientist, came up with a theory that was commonly referred to as the "rating and dating" complex. He too said that dating was not about love or marriage but about competition among youth to see who could get the most dates and thus be the most popular. E. S. Turner's book, *A History of Courting* (1954), describes Waller's theory this way: "The men who rated were those who could afford a car, fancy dinners, etc. The women who were sought after were those who were rated as popular by virtue of their ability to date different men three to four times a week. Women were also rated through their ability to adhere to the current standards of beauty held up by popular culture."

Of course, many others disagreed with these analyses at the time, arguing that the new system of dating was better than what existed before (the "let's meet in my parlor" version), because it was an educational process. It allowed young people to shop around, to try out a few different flavors until they found something they really liked.

However, even today, not all cultures are on board with the concept. For example, Amira, an Indian woman I spoke to who lives in North America but went back to India to marry a man her parents had chosen for her, puts it this way: "At least with arranged marriages, girls know they will get married, so they don't have to worry or compete." No stress. When they are old enough, their parents simply choose a suitable boy.

"I'd rather have my parents choose for me," Amira continues. "They have more experience than I do."

Obviously not all Indian women feel the same way, but it does remind us that while we often take dating as a given, it is only one way of doing things.

In some ways, not much has changed since the early 1900s in the World o' Dating. Sure, we may write our love letters on e-mail and do our courting on telepersonals, but the basic concept has remained the same: hunt around to find someone you like, hang out, get to know each other a little, see if it clicks – and if it doesn't, hunt around to find someone you like, hang out…

But in other ways, plenty has changed, as you will see throughout the pages of this book. You might say that, in some ways, dating as we once knew it has become a little outdated.

# Dating Defined

In this day and age, our definition of dating is a bit hard to pin down. Here's how some of the people I spoke to defined it:

- "A date is an elaborate interview process that allows you to classify a relationship with someone as partner, friend, acquaintance or someone you want nothing to do with."

- "It's anything that has the potential of ending in sexual contact, whether it be a peck with possible relationship connotations or a good hard fuck."

- "A non-platonic outing or meeting with someone of the opposite sex (or personal preference)."

- "It's a way of getting to know someone you find at least vaguely attractive before entering the commitment of a relationship."

- "Dating is a tough assignment with so many things to remember, while not stepping on any toes."

- "A date is when you meet someone and say, 'Do you want to go for a drink or something?' and then you sit down, talk about your life and try to come off as interesting as you can in half an hour in order to get to the next level. It's a bit like playing a video game."

- "It's the first time you're alone with someone. You've met the person at parties or with friends but now you're alone and that's a date. You might not call it a date but that's a date."

- "I tend to end up in bed with people before I realize it's a date."

- "There are two types of dating: there's dating as part of the hunt and dating to find a mate."

- "I don't hear the word 'dating' very often. It seems to me people get right into a relationship and there's nothing in between."

- "Dating seems to be what I call it when I go out with men I have no interest in."

- "A date is a protective sort of structure for spending time with somebody where you don't have to feel obligated to become involved with them. There's a beginning, a middle and an end. You know there's an end."

- "Dating is like shopping. You have to look around until you find something that suits you."

- "What is a date? If the person actually shows up."

- "Dating is foreplay!"

# If There Are So Many Single People, Why Can't I Get a Date?

My parents lived down the road from each other when they were kids growing up in the country. They walked to school together, dated as teens and got married. Simple.

These days, you're lucky if you even know your neighbor. Especially if you live in the city. No wonder there are more single people than ever. According to Statistics Canada, the number of single people grew 11 percent between 1991 and 1995. That's almost twice the population increase.

Why?

According to those who think about these things, singleness really started to catch on in the seventies, once we got over the Cleavers and came down off the brown acid.

Since the seventies we've been staying single longer. In 1972, the average age that women got married was 21. Now it's 26. Today, the average marrying age for men is 27, compared to 24 in 1972.

Divorce has also become more and more acceptable since the seventies. (Used to be you were pretty much ostracized from the community if you got divorced.) As a result, 40 percent of people who jump on the marriage bandwagon now jump off and get divorced, creating a lot of newly single people out there.

So, you may ask, if there's so many single people out there, why is it so hard to find a good date? Well, the chances of two people finding each other at a point when they are both feeling good about themselves, are not totally bound up in their last relationship and are ready to embark on something new are slim at best. These days there are also all kinds of other factors against us.

For one, many of us hardly stay in one place long enough to meet anyone. In my parents' day, they were lucky if they traveled outside of their small Dutch village. Now people move around all the time; they change cities, even countries, like underwear. Being further flung, I think we've lost some sense of community. In the city, everyone's afraid to talk to each other. And the suburbs are full of already-hitched couples.

We're more focused on our careers. Statistics show that we work 164 hours more a year than we did 25 years ago. Who has time to date? As a result, dating gets placed lower on the priority scale.

We're pickier. We want a perfect emotional, intellectual and physical match, and we're simply not willing to settle for less. Not that we should. It's just that getting all our needs met can be a real challenge. "Women have many more needs than they used to, and so have men," offers Ann-Marie, a 33-year-old journalist who knows what she wants and does her damnedest to get it. "Before, the cliché was that men needed to feel that they're making their means in the world. Women needed to feel secure. To have a home. Now we both want both. It's as if we've each become both woman and man. You feel like you're dating a foursome."

"I think it's exciting, actually," says John, a 32-year-old choreographer. "People are more complicated than ever, and everyone has different interests and needs. On one level, it's more stressful, but on another, it's an exciting challenge. I think that this is the best time in history for dating, ever."

Of course, John's optimism might have something to do with the fact that he's freshly single after a two-year relationship. He's still got that glow of newfound freedom about him. Talk to him in six months and see how much he likes dating then.

## Date from Hell

I was about 18 when I asked this girl out on a date. I dressed up, borrowed my dad's car, drove to her house and rang the bell. Her parents answered, led me to the kitchen and then left me there while they watched *Dallas* (hey, it was the eighties). Then in walked this yappy little poodle. I started to pet it and it bit me, right on the hand, and it got its tooth stuck in my palm. I was freaking out trying to shake this dog off my hand, and suddenly I smacked it against the fridge and, I kid you not, the dog broke its neck, fell off my hand and dropped dead on the kitchen floor. Then this girl's father came back into the kitchen to pour himself a drink, and I explained what happened. He looked at the dog for a second, then looked at me, then back at the dog, and he said, "I always hated that fucking dog anyway." Then he picked it up, put it in a plastic bag and threw it in the backyard. "Listen," he said, "if I were you, I wouldn't mention this. It's just between me and you, okay? Now go on out, and you kids have a good time. I'll tell her when she gets back."

Some of us are less enamored with dating. "Here's how I sum up the dating scene: grim!" says Jennifer, a 30-year-old filmmaker who is clearly feeling a little cynical about dating at the moment. "Men are all either too serious, gay, attached, stupid or boring."

And double the difficulty if you're divorced and back on the scene. Not only are you rusty, but you have the "damaged goods" stigma to deal with, making dating a particularly fun challenge. And if you're really lucky, you have kids. Divorced people with kids, or single mothers, not only have to find a suitable date for themselves, but they also have to find someone their kids won't spit on.

The fact that the whole act of dating is also not as clear-cut as it once was doesn't help either. I think for a lot of us, even the term "dating" conjures up images of *Happy Days* and soda fountains. Dating is seen at best as quaint, at worst, kinda schlocky and uncool.

Nowadays, a date is more like, "Oh, look, somehow we ended up at the same table in this cafe. I guess this is sort of, kind of, maybe, a date. Or not. Whatever." We're so ambivalent that most of the time we're too scared to even call it a date. We don't want to formally "date" someone because what if it doesn't work out? Why make ourselves vulnerable? And if we've been burned a few times before, we're even less willing to take a chance.

"I hate dating," says Dawn, a 36-year-old TV producer who was in an eight-year relationship but recently found herself back in the dating saddle. "I take back everything negative I ever said about jumping drunkenly into bed with someone and then starting a relationship. Frankly, I think that's a much better way to go."

Okay, so it gets a little discouraging once in a while. You can't let it get to you. No one wants to go out with a grump. I'm not saying you have to be delirious about dating, but a positive attitude will go far.

## Setting a Bad Example

You can't really blame us for having such a hard time with it all. We haven't exactly had tons of guidance. Most of the people I spoke to said their parents gave them pretty much zero advice.

"One night, when I was 21, I was on my way out on a date," recalls Nathan, a 31-year-old, self-proclaimed sensitive guy who works in advertising. "My mother says to me, 'I just hope you're being responsible.' I realized about six months later that she was talking about sex. That was about the extent of her advice."

Jeez, with that kind of training, how are we supposed to get it right?

Twenty-eight-year-old Amy comes from a very traditional family that discouraged any dating activity at all. "I dated anyway, but I just never brought any of my dates home, and they never came to pick me up at my place. I'd always meet them. It was all very furtive, which sort of added to the excitement but really was a bit of a shame. I would have liked to have been able to show my dates to my sisters and my mom, just to get some feedback and advice."

And, with so many of us being children of divorce, we don't even have the example of our parents to work with. Never mind how screwed up we are by the divorce or how we had to watch our newly divorced parents date and make the same mistakes all over again. And even if we're not completely dysfunctional, chances are the people we meet are. No wonder a simple request like, "Want to go for coffee?" sends them screaming from the room, lugging their baggage with them.

Without any parental guidance, we did what most kids did: turned to TV or the movies (which sends us even further from reality). Next thing you know, we're looking for someone like Matt Damon, the screwed-up but hunky genius in the movie *Good Will Hunting,* who works out all his childhood issues with a good cry and a big hug from Robin Williams and then gives up his dream job to drive a beat-up old car across the country to be with us. Most of us are lucky if we can find someone who even has a job.

And again, even if you've learned to resist the fairy tale, there's no guarantee the people you date have.

Add to all this the fact that we're stuck with all the leftovers of previous generations' dating problems – AIDS and STDs, for example – and suddenly something as simple as dinner and a movie with someone is a pretty daunting proposal.

Maybe "dating is dead," as one person wrote. Or maybe the idea needs a little updating. "It lacks imagination," 18-year-old Sandy says. "It's just been so done so many zillions of times that it's no longer meaningful."

It's only taken us 100 years to invent and then completely screw up the concept of dating as we know it. Maybe we'll come up with a new system in the next century. Lining everyone up and pairing them off is one method I've been tossing around. For now, as John said to me, "It may be a flawed system, but it's the only one we've got."

With that in mind, I offer you this guide to dating. I don't have all the answers, but I've got a few (as well as some pretty good guesses). I've also tried to keep a healthy sense of humor about it all, because, God knows, you gotta laugh about this shit once in a while. But, most wonderfully, what you'll find in this guide are the voices and the experiences of people like you, people just trying to get a date. Consider it a bit of friendly advice from your comrades on the frontlines.

# Shop 'Til You Drop

## Are We Still Looking for Love in All the Usual Places?

We can probably all agree on one thing about dating: it requires two people. And because sitting next to someone on the bus does not qualify as a date, this means you have to make an effort to meet someone you'd like to date.

"But I don't know where to meet people," all the single people whine. Well, truth is, it's easy to meet people — they're everywhere. How to meet an attractive, interesting person you might want to tongue wrestle with is a different story.

Sadly, however, this does mean you have to turn off the TV, get up off the couch and go look.

"But where do I look?" you groan.

Thanks to the spirit of free enterprise, there are plenty of folks eager to help. From personal ads to dating agencies, telepersonals to matchmakers, and now the Internet, getting people together is big business.

Of course, there are still the good old-fashioned ways, like stumbling home together from the bar, stumbling home together from the office party or letting a friend introduce you to "this reeeally ni-i-ice guy" she knows.

So, technically yes, there are plenty of ways to meet people out there. Making any of them work for you is the hard part.

Let's take a look at the pros and cons of some of the most common ways to meet people.

## School Daze

When you're in school, you almost have to go out of your way *not* to meet people. University is quite literally a breeding ground for young, horny, single people with too much time on their hands. And since you all share the same bad cafeteria food, you have plenty to bond over. The fact that you spend half the time in a drunken haze doesn't hurt either.

As Marie from Edmonton wrote in response to my dating questionnaire, the best place to meet people is in a university residence: "You get to know people really fast since you're in such close quarters. A week of rez dating is worth at least a month of the 'regular' variety."

Hey, once he's seen you in your jammies with the feet in them, there's not much left to hide.

But you can only put off graduation for so long (some are better at this than others, I've noticed). If you haven't hooked up with someone by the time you're outta there, the "school mating" method is pretty much history, and you've got to move on to the next tactic.

## All In a Day's Work

One of the positive side effects of women entering the workforce way back when was that it created a whole new venue to meet people. Suddenly, you could potentially meet a mate on company time.

These days, however, with sexual harassment paranoia and the fact that, unlike back at university, you can no longer wow 'em with your ability to knock back 15 "Sex on the Beach" shooters without throwing up, work has become less date-friendly.

Some companies in the U.S. have gone so far as to ban office romance. Others have hired labor lawyers to draft agreements regulating it. As yet, this practice is illegal in Canada, so if you move fast, you can still make the moves on that hunka burning love in the next cubicle.

Mind you, not all workplaces are crawling with potential dates. Also unlike university, most work environments are not full of young, single people. More corporate environments tend to be full of settled, married types (who got lucky at school), so unless you to want to bust up a family, you're out of luck. Never mind the risk you take with your professional reputation in these highly competitive, "if you don't wanna do it there are plenty of people who would" days.

Then again, if you're, let's say, a woman engineer and you're straight, odds are probably still in your favor in terms of available men. If you're a straight male engineer, you're kinda screwed (or not, as the case may be). If you're a gay man, you'll probably be frustrated because most of your colleagues are straight, and if you're a lesbian, you'll also be frustrated because you'll inevitably have a crush on the one other chick engineer in the firm and spend all your time convincing yourself she's a closet-case.

Despite all this, plenty of people still say work is one of the best places to meet people. Hey, you're guaranteed at least one thing in common. And like I said, some work environments offer better odds than others. One straight guy I talked to had this to say about his work in musical theater: "The great thing is that there are tons of gay guys and lots of attractive women who are all complaining bitterly about how all the guys in the theater are gay. So when there's one straight guy, they're on him like flies to…well, you know!"

Or you could be like me, a writer who spends her days working at home, alone. Eventually even the old, bald guy at the corner store where I buy my newspaper starts to look good.

## Friendly Gestures

The number-one way to meet people, hands down, according to most of the people who wrote or spoke to me, is through friends.

As Scott from Winnipeg wrote, "there's less weirdo potential." I'm not so sure (my friends know some weird people), but certainly meeting people through friends does seem the most natural and effortless way to meet someone. If your friend introduces you to one of their single friends, you can innocently chat, suss them out and proceed (or not) from there. No need to commit to anything on the spot. You can milk your friend for info later and find out if there's mutual interest or any history of ax-murdering in your potential date's family. Then casually arrange to "run" into each other "by coincidence" at a strategically arranged dinner party at your friend's house.

The worst, however, is when your coupled friends decide who they think you should date. In other words, someone your best friend would go out with if she were single, but she can't, so she foists him on you so she can date him vicariously. Then you get to watch them hit it off all night while you go home empty-handed. Or, better yet, your friends invite you to a dinner party and tell you they'll invite their other pathetic single friend because they're certain the two of you would be "perfect together." Inevitably, he's the guy with the bad breath and the conversation skills of a slug.

"My friend did that," says 31-year-old Diane, a writer and self-described "cynical, bitter single woman." "She calls me and says, 'Come over. This guy's over at our house and he's a friend of my husband's and blah blah blah...'

"So I went over and I'm thinking, 'Oh God, that's who you think I'd be interested in? I'm so not interested! You so don't get my taste!' The worst thing was that I don't think he was interested in me either, and we both knew why I was there, so we were like, 'Hi, nice to meet you. LET ME OUT OF HERE!'"

## Party On!

If dinner parties are a little too high-pressure and intimate, a full-on house party is another oft-cited meeting place. But you have to get the right formula to throw a good "mingling" party, says Nathan.

"It has to be a good combination of people you know, some of their friends and some people you don't know," explains Nathan. "That way, most people are connected in some way, but there are a few wild cards in the bunch, just to keep it fresh. And it's best to keep it kind of small – 20 or 30 people, max." This way, you always have an opening line: "So who do you know here?"

If you're not comfortable with party small talk, look for someone doing something unusual and you're guaranteed a conversation topic.

"I met Anne at a party," says Elizabeth, a 36-year-old lesbian playwright who says she hates parties. "She'd just quit smoking, and I saw her sitting crankily in the corner squinting at the write-up on a nicotine patch. I found her attractive, so I walked up and made a comment about her choice of literature."

## Bar None

Everyone says they hate the bar scene. As the old saying goes: "Every relationship that starts in a bar ends in a bar." I suppose that's why we all wait in line in flimsy dress-up clothes, waiting to get into them. Somehow, despite our contempt, this ancient, tried-and-true singles tradition is alive and well.

That's because, without church or community dances to bring us together, bars are one of the few places you can go where people socialize without the "I'm trying to meet someone" stigma. Plus they serve alcohol. Nothing like a little booze to open us up, make ourselves and others seem interesting and interested. That is, until it turns us into a bundle of slobbering, indiscriminate hormones.

I imagine future anthropologists tracing the mating rituals of humans in the late 20th century as follows: "Humans could be observed in large groups at something they called a bar, sucking a golden liquid from brown glass bottles. After they had consumed copious amounts of the golden liquid, they attempted to capture each other's attention with lewd body language, bad pick-up lines or offers of small glasses of liquid that they tossed back in one gulp. At the end of the evening, the lucky ones paired off with a new mate and could be seen awkwardly entangled in various corners of the bar and, in some cases, leaving together. Others stumbled home, accompanied only by a slice of a rather greasy food substance they called 'pizza.'"

Different types of bars offer different cruising experiences. Downtown is where you usually find the really blatant pick-up joints, the kind in which the dance floor is basically a display case, and brushing up against someone on the way to the bathroom is akin to an invitation to take them home. Not exactly subtle, but effective if you're merely looking to get laid.

The loud music in dance clubs makes it hard to strike up a conversation, but there's nothing like a bunch of hot, sweaty bodies bumping and grinding to get the pheromones cranked. As Don, one of my respondents, wrote, "Since I learned to dance, my sex life has increased tenfold."

Poser bars full of beautiful scenesters with great clothes and nothing to say are good if you're a beautiful person with great clothes and nothing to say. Otherwise, they just make you feel like a poverty victim looking for handouts. And it's hell cutting through all that attitude.

My fave bars are the loungey or pub-like places where you can sit with friends, catch someone's eye across the room, table hop or find yourself seated with people you don't know. It's a bit like being in your parents' rec room at your first mixed party as a teenager, and someone has spiked the punch.

No matter where you go, the key is not to look like you're dying for some. I still have a little cupid pin that a woman once gave me. She came up with this idea that single people could wear these pins to let others know they are available. "Why not save yourself the five bucks and write 'desperate loser' in black marker on your forehead?" I thought. No surprise, that little venture didn't catch on.

There's no need to advertise. The key to the bar scene is to be cool and discreet, and not to expect to find the man or woman of your dreams. Because, as your friends tell you over and over until you want to choke their adorable little necks, you never meet someone when you're looking too hard. I know they're right, but it's still annoying.

The bartender can be a pivotal figure in the bar cruising game. He or she can be a buffer if you're alone. He can give you the poop on certain customers and even play cupid if you give him a target. But don't get your hopes up too high.

"Anything meaningful is a long shot," admits Philippe, a bartender at a notorious downtown Montreal "meet market." "It happens, but a meaningful commitment is not the main attraction. Men just want to get laid, and if something more comes out of it, bonus."

And don't kid yourself, women are just as bad. One woman I know had a card made up with her name and phone number, which she handed out to men she fancied.

As 28-year-old Martin, a student and seasoned barfly, says, "You're not looking for long-term when you go to a bar. You just want something you won't have to bag before you fuck."

Charming. And you wonder why people are disillusioned with the bar scene?

## Join the Club

I know, I know, it sounds cheesy to suggest joining a club or taking a class as a way to meet people. And personally, I don't know anyone who has met this way. But it seems like it should work. Maybe part of the problem is that women are the only ones getting these kinds of suggestions from all the stupid *Cosmo* articles they've read.

"Any class I've taken has been 80 percent women," laments 30-year-old Carol, a graphic designer who decided to act on these suggestions from women's magazines. Perhaps it could have something to do with the classes she's taken. Face it, you're just not gonna get a lot of studly men in an aromatherapy course. But now you know where all the babes are, guys.

A course in something challenging and unusual might be good, because you'd have plenty of new material to discuss with an attractive classmate. And even if you didn't meet someone, you'd now be a better person for having learned how to make an origami pot holder.

Taking a course in a physical activity is another option. Watching all those fit bodies kick-boxing or rock climbing is a good way to jump-start your hormones and get into shape. You gotta be into it, though. If you're a couch potato who hates the cold and you take snowboarding lessons just to meet people, you might come off a little suspect.

If you want to meet more intellectual, sensitive, artist types, try a writing workshop or create a book club of single friends.

Or take up music. Several North American symphony orchestras have introduced singles nights. (Even the upper crust is getting in on the singles action.) For the price of a ticket, you join a bunch of single classical music lovers for a concert. Sometimes they even throw in a lecture and a snack to get things really hopping.

Joining a club or organization that is formed around a common interest is great because, well, you find people with common interests, at least one of the elements of a good relationship. Like 34-year-old Deborah, a restaurant owner who met her boyfriend at fetish night. He liked to be whipped and she found herself thrilled to whip him. A perfect match.

Some clubs are organized around certain physical traits that might hinder your ability to find an appropriate date: Tall Club International (TCI), for example. TCI has more than 2,000 members in 54 chapters throughout North America. It's a social/singles/lobby club – a place to meet and hang out with people with whom you literally see eye-to-eye and fight for things like longer broom handles and clothes that fit.

Rick barely makes the minimum at 6'2½", but he joined the Tall Club in the hopes of finding someone whose eyes he could stare into and whose head wouldn't be buried in his belly button when they danced. "A lot of tall guys like to date tall women," Rick says. "It's just a better fit. You don't get neck cramps trying to kiss."

Volunteering is another way to get yourself in the game. So what if your goodwill isn't entirely unselfish? Just consider putting an end to your single status as part of the cause. When you volunteer, you'll need someone to show you what to do, and hey, why not that cute chick with the tight "Save the Dolphins" T-shirt? Again, try to at least pick a cause you give somewhat of a shit about. You don't want to launch into a tirade about cruelty to animals with the cutie at the Vegetarian Volleyball Charity Tournament and suddenly realize you have burger breath.

## Nice Melons!

Again, women's mags are always going on about how you can meet people *everywhere!* Hang out at your local soup kitchen! Or maybe that woman peeing in the bathroom stall next to yours is your dream girl! Or, who knows, that guy asking you for change could change your life!

Seriously, though, these mags are full of it. The suggestion that places like the gym, the supermarket and the laundromat are crawling with potential dates is a little hard to take. What do you do, shuffle up to someone in the produce section and say, "Hey, nice melons"?

When I go to the gym, I'm there to work out. And when I go to the laundromat, I'm in my "only thing clean because I never wear them because they're so ugly" stretch pants and have bed-head.

I know you really *can* meet people anywhere. But the "going to the supermarket dressed to the nines looking for it" aspect of it makes me cringe. However, Ann-Marie says she keeps her radar on at all times. Then she's open to it if she happens to stumble upon Mr. Possibility on the bus. Not a bad attitude.

The key, she says, is to be bold and not to expect too much. "I'm not scared," Ann-Marie asserts. "I've asked people out on buses, in gyms. The thing is, I'm willing to deal with the consequences if I don't get a response."

So just how do you approach somebody on a bus? (I had to ask.)

"It's not so much approaching them," Ann-Marie says. "But you might happen to be sitting by someone and talking to them and you think they're cute. So you suss them out. I don't usually go so far as to ask someone out on sight, although I did once. But I hadn't been laid for a long time…It was more out of sexual desperation."

I'm beginning to wonder if I should take the bus more often. Nathan also met a woman that way. "I was at the bus stop and I asked if she had the time. Luckily she didn't notice I was wearing a watch," he says. "We started talking and ended up chatting the whole bus ride. We ended up taking the bus together two or three days a week. Then she invited me to a club launch, but I realized that, out of the context of the bus, we didn't have a whole lot in common."

There ya go.

Art galleries are another oft-cited meeting spot. Most public museums have a free or half-price night and, I have to admit, I've gone on these nights and the place is crawling with people who are eyeing more than the art.

"Looking at an art show gives you something to talk about," says Mark, a 25-year-old aspiring filmmaker and art-lover. "You can walk up to a complete stranger and say, 'Isn't it interesting how Monet used those teeny specs of paint to recreate light?' or 'What do you think of Cubism? I don't know, my five-year-old kid could do better.'"

Libraries and bookstores are also pretty cruise-friendly. Books, like art, make a handy prop. "Oh, I've read that *Dating* book too. Isn't Josey Vogels a brilliant writer?"

# And Now for Something a Little Different

Tired of bars and parties? Some people I spoke to had a few alternative suggestions on where to meet people.

- "Join a cult," says Mark, our art-lover. "Sure, the whole suicide pact can be a bit of a drag, but it's so romantic: 'Let's kill ourselves together.'"

- "At a funeral," suggests Carol, who met someone at her aunt's funeral.

- "Dog walking," suggests Ann-Marie. "I met this guy in the park who just got a new dog. I showed him how to pick up the poop – you know, you put the plastic bag over your hand..." How romantic, they picked up dog shit together.

- "At church," says Deborah. Wow, just like the old days. "I was in Montreal, staring up at the ceiling of the Notre Dame Basilica, and this guy ended up giving me a personal tour that lasted long after we left the church."

- "In a hospital emergency room," says Martin. "I had food poisoning and this woman came over and said I looked so bad, she felt sorry for me. She ended up rubbing my back while I waited."

- "On a ski hill," says Ann-Marie, obviously a mine of information when it comes to meeting people in unusual places. "I couldn't find the trail I was looking for. I asked this guy and he ended up skiing down with me. Then we warmed up in the chalet."

See, you just never know.

# The Meet Market

As I said earlier, if you're having trouble meeting people through the regular channels, there are plenty of people out there willing to help. For a fee, of course. Hitching people up is officially a growth industry. There are even trade shows to prove it.

I was at something called the Singles' Lifestyles Show in Toronto a while back. The entire floor of the Metro Toronto Convention Centre was devoted to services for single people. "It certainly brings new meaning to the term 'meet market,'" I thought, as I watched a solitary, obviously very optimistic, person skating around and around a makeshift roller rink. A sign above him said, "Roll into someone's heart!"

It's tough not to buy into the single-equals-loser stereotype when perky women with shellacked blond hair are grinning maniacally and handing out brochures for a boat cruise where "IT'LL ALL BE SINGLES, HONEY!" Terrifying.

Even the Christians were in on the act. Or, if you can't find Holy Matrimony through The Singles Christian Network, there was The Single Gourmet, a suspiciously foodless "social network...for people who like meeting people." The club organizes parties and getaways for its members. An upcoming bus trip to Montreal was described as "just like a trip to Paris, but without the jet lag."

Do people really need all this help to meet someone? We're certainly being convinced we do. Single people have become a huge market, and it seems there are no bounds when it comes to cashing in on our loneliness. I read about one service in the U.S. where single people could hire a "date" and, at the end of the evening, the client got a report card that rated them on how good a date they were and where they needed to improve.

Even if you aren't that desperate, there are plenty of places you can spend money trying to find a date. Most folks go for the standard services: personal ads, telepersonals, dating agencies or the Internet. Even good old-fashioned matchmaking is still alive and well. There's a guy in Montreal who stands on a street corner and hands out his card to single-looking folks (c'mon, you can just tell), promising he can find their match – for a price, needless to say.

Other matchmaking services have updated their approach, offering advice on dating etiquette as well as relationship coaching. Oh, excuse me, they don't call them "matchmakers" anymore. They're now called "relationship consultants."

Not everyone is comfortable soliciting outside help to meet someone. "It just feels so desperate," they complain, downing their third martini and waiting for their dream date to fall off the next bar stool and into their lap. But plenty of people use these services, and they have plenty to say about them, both good and bad. With the glut of services available, you might as well take advantage of their experience.

## Getting Personals

Advertising for a date is not a new phenomenon. Pretty much as soon as there were newspapers, there were personal ads. According to E. S. Turner's *A History of Courting*, "As the [18th] century progressed, the unscrupulous, the timorous, and the idle began to use the advertising columns of the newspapers in an effort to find suitable (and suitably endowed) partners in matrimony."

And there was none of this "I like candlelit dinners and walks along the beach" crap. They got straight to the point: "An agreeable gentleman between 40 and 50 is desirous of marrying an agreeable gentlewoman with 800£ or 1,000£ in ready money and would settle on her a very good estate of 200£ a year." Another gent was seeking "a woman with soft lips, expressive eyes, sweet breath." Yet another had nice tits on his wish-list: "bosom full, plump, firm and white."

Personals really took off when the telephone got in on the act, allowing you to both read about and listen to the person before you got anywhere near them. According to the 1994 *Consumer's Guide to Dating and Introduction Services* by Peter Crocker, in one year alone a company called Direct Response Marketing (one of the biggest telepersonals companies, responsible for a lot of the telepersonals you see in the free cultural weeklies found in most North American cities) received more than 10 million calls and reported sales of more than $163 million.

While advertising for a mate doesn't seem very romantic, for some it's practical. "I started using telepersonals because I live in Toronto, where people don't talk to each other," Carol says. "I've traveled around and I notice that men are bolder in other places. I was in Paris once, wearing a miniskirt, and a man walked right up to me and told me I had nice kneecaps. I admired his directness. That wouldn't happen here." (Amazing what a French accent lets you get away with.)

For Carol, taking out a personal ad is a way of taking action when she's not getting any action any other way. "I don't want to be alone all the time, so using the telepersonals gives me a sense of control over my situation, like I'm doing something about it," she says.

It can also leave a hefty phone bill. While some telepersonals let you listen to ads for free, you have to pay every time you respond to an ad. "I tried them again recently," says Carol. "I answered four ads, heard back from two of them and didn't end up going out with any of them. And I spent $100!"

One of the biggest complaints from people who have tried personal ads is encountering false advertising. "I found telepersonals to be a big waste of time because so many women lied about their appearance," says Richard, a 33-year-old artist.

"I met so many 300-pound women who hadn't mentioned that little detail when they were describing themselves. So here you've invested all this time placing an ad, responding to them, picking up messages, talking to people and arranging to meet. And then you show up for your first meeting, take one

## Date from Hell

I had a free coupon from Man-Line, the gay telepersonals service. I never placed my own ad, I just listened to a whole bunch. Well, one ad in particular caught my attention. It was in French, English and German. I responded and chatted on the phone with this guy a bit. He had a really good phone voice and he was hilarious. But when we met in person, I realized he had this nervous laughter thing. Every time he'd finish a sentence or make a joke he'd say, "Tsk, well anyway! Heh, heh, heh." It drove me nuts. He asked me to go back to his place for a bit, and for some reason I agreed. As it turned out, he lived in a basement apartment way out in the suburbs. Have you ever tried to seduce someone in a small, faux-wood-paneled, semi-furnished basement in the 'burbs? It's like being back in your parents' rec room! Needless to say, it didn't work out.

look at them and go 'yech.' But you can't say that, so you go through with it, put in some time, say how nice it was to meet you – and get the hell outta there. It's a lot of work."

Obviously Richard has yet to learn about the delights of ample women. I wonder how women feel about his scrawny little butt.

Anyhow, women aren't the only liars. Lise, a 37-year-old divorced accountant, responded to an ad from a man who described himself as "tall and slim and interested in music." Turns out he lived down the hall from her.

"We recognized each other's voices, and suddenly it dawns on me that I pass this guy in my building all the time. Then I'm thinking, 'Holy shit.' I mean, you can smell this man from my apartment. He doesn't bathe, he's your classic computer geek with pants up to here…and the hair! And I'm thinking, 'tall and slim'? Give me a break!

"I had to dance my way out of it. I said, 'You know what, I guess we should both just laugh this off.' And he said, 'Actually, I've really wanted to ask you out.' I said I never dated people in the same building or people at work. 'So, uhhh, how about I call you back next week?' Thank God I never saw him again. Luckily, he eventually moved out."

Another common complaint is that so many of the ads sound the same. How do you differentiate between one outdoor-loving person and the next? If you decide to go this route, it's more strategic to be specific.

"Mention some weird and quirky things about yourself, or weird and quirky things that you like, and be really specific," says our fat-phobic friend Richard. "Because the more general you are the less likely you are to attract someone who's interested in the same things."

Like the ad Elizabeth told me she'd take out. "Seeking girl with cottage. Please send photo of cottage." Right to the point, you know?

The other big problem with personals is that there's no guarantee that even if you don't go "yech" at first sight, you won't go "yech" 10 minutes into your coffee date because you realize there's absolutely no chemistry.

Sam, a 35-year-old photographer, says he once wrote to a guy in the personal ads. "He phoned me, and we went out on a couple of dates, but it became glaringly apparent that chemistry is so complex – 100 words in the newspaper ain't gonna do it. It's just too difficult."

But it's not all outdoor-lovers, computer geeks and incompatible body types. There are some advantages to the personals. For instance, I just found out that an old friend of mine is about to marry someone she met through an ad. Trust me, this is not a woman who has a hard time getting a date. She's the last person I would expect to use this method. But she said she got tired of all the immature guys she seemed to end up dating. She took out a personal ad as a way to force herself to try dating someone different. It worked.

Also, for those who aren't so comfortable approaching people at parties or in bars, the personals lay out the introduction rules for you. You both know what you're there for. As Sam describes it, "You arrange to have a drink so you can sort of sniff each other's asses and move on, and that's what you do."

The other advantage is that you get a chance to assert your personality before the person sees you. That gives physical attraction less of a head start. And even if you don't hit it off, you gain experience meeting people and learn more about what you do and don't want. If you're lucky, you might even make a few new friends — and that can't be so bad. But there is no denying the weirdo potential when you accept a date sight-unseen. A few words of caution: Be sure to meet in a public place, and don't give anyone your address before you meet them.

## Dating Service with a Smile

While the telepersonals can set you back a few bucks, dating agencies are an even bigger investment. You can pay dating agencies thousands of dollars to come up with more tailor-made and, theoretically, more successful matches for you. But buyer beware. A higher price doesn't always mean better service.

Tina, a 36-year-old divorced school teacher, was suspicious when the guy the dating agency arranged for her to meet kept avoiding their encounter. She really began to wonder when — after they finally did meet — she called the guy at home to thank him for the date and realized there was another woman there. When she asked him if he was married or living with someone, he wouldn't answer.

As she had been instructed to do, she told the agency that her encounter hadn't worked out. She voiced her suspicions that she had been set up and that the guy was perhaps even working for the company. The company told her they'd check it out. Six months and 252 unreturned phone calls later, she realized she'd been had – and they still owed her two more dates. The company eventually closed down, the owner was investigated for fraud charges and this poor woman was out more than $1,000.

Nothing makes you feel more pathetic than getting robbed blind by a dating agency while seeking a blind date.

Most dating agencies – or introduction services, as they prefer to be called – arrange tailor-made "introductions" for you based on a slew of personality and psychological tests they put you through when you join. I went to check it out for myself and, I have to admit, I was impressed. It all seemed very scientific, with plenty of pyramids and graphs to represent the cycles and patterns of relationships.

The whole shtick was based on the notion that relationships are nine parts compatibility and one part chemistry. If you're like me, you look for the one part chemistry first and worry about all that silly nine parts compatibility stuff later. Here, they did it the other way around. They set you up with compatible people – people with similar personality traits and interests. Eventually, one of these compatible people will also come with chemistry. *Et voilà,* perfect match.

For busy people who don't have the time to go through thousands of personal ads and are tired of the bar scene, an agency may be helpful. And, if they're not crooked, dating agencies can work.

"My sister went to a dating service because they had a special promotion – no charge for women," says Karen, a 30-year-old radio producer who has no patience for organized matchmaking herself. "She spent a couple of hours in an interview. Soon after, they called her, and she went on a date with this guy. She got married to him two months later. They've been together four years now, but she didn't tell us how they met until the wedding. She was too embarrassed."

Again with the stigma.

# Dating Service Savvy

If you do decide to try out an "introduction service," there are a few things to consider:

- Do your research. Some have better reps than others. And don't take their word for it. Check with the Consumer Protection Office and suss out the service's record before you hand over any cash.

- Don't think that because it's a big, well-known company or name, it's necessarily better. Many of the big agencies sell franchises, like the one Tina used. You're often better off choosing a small, local company that employs matchmakers with plenty of experience under their belt. They operate on intuition and often have a good match in mind the moment they lay eyes on you.

- If something looks too good to be true, it probably is. According to Canada's Consumer Protection folks, 63 percent of commercial matchmaking services go under in the first two years.

- Go through your contract with a fine-tooth comb. There are lots of little things they can stick in there to get around their claim to guarantee you a match. For example, they can say you're not a worthy candidate if you have kids, are ethnic, etc. (I'm serious, some of them do this.)

- It's not cheap. You may want to exhaust some other routes before making this kind of investment.

- Check out their clients' demographics. Does it match what you're looking for?

- Try to get a deal. You can bargain, especially with the bigger agencies. And while you're reading the fine print, make sure you won't be surprised later on with any additional costs they "forgot to mention."

## Cruising On-Line

With its chat rooms, special-interest forums and more matchmaking sites that you can shake a stick at, the Internet has become to the nineties what the singles bar was to the seventies.

The cool thing, of course, is that while the impression you create in a bar is influenced by your outfit and whether or not you're having a good hair day, you can cruise cyberspace in the privacy of your own home in your sweats. In other words, you can look ugly as sin and be a glam-babe on-line.

The biggest problem, however, is that if and when you do decide to meet a special cybersomeone in the flesh, there's a good chance the electronic sparks you created on-line won't fly in real life.

But if you wanna look for love on-line, there are plenty of places to go. Rich Gosse is the president of American Singles, the largest non-profit singles organization worldwide, with members in 96 countries and one of the most extensive on-line web sites for singles. He says that more than 1.5 million personal ads circulate in cyberspace at any given time.

Many web sites, like Gosse's www.cupidnet.com, group together a list of sites offering something for everyone. A sampling of the 100-plus sites listed at www.SingleSites.com, for example, includes: "Antonio's Beautiful Russian & Ukraine Women," "A Singles Christian Network," "KinkyContacts.com (If you want the REAL THING, the hottest contacts, the hottest times, get Kinky!)," "Dates-R-Us (A cutting-edge cyber-dating system)," "1st Bulgarian Singles," "CIAMC (The Crimean International Acquaintance & Marriage Club)," "Jewish Singles LoveLink," "Large and Lovely Connections (Catering to adults of size and their admirers)," "Filipina Dream Girls," "Suddenly Single" (for adults over 50 who find themselves, well, suddenly single) and "South Africa Love Center Dating Center." You get the idea.

Let's just take a closer look at one of these. Clark and Kathy started A Singles Christian Network in 1991. When I interviewed them — by e-mail, of course — they told me that, since its origin, the SCN has been responsible for more than 300 marriages. It obviously helps to have the Big Guy in the Sky on your side.

Clark says people use his service because "dating in the nineties is difficult for Christians." Bombarded from every quarter with issues contradicting their faith, conservative Christians feel especially "left out," he says. "They don't want to go to the bars to meet someone, and sexual casualness is all too popular. If they don't have a large singles group at church, where do they go? So we provide a simple mechanism for them to find and meet that person they are seeking."

Personals on the Internet have an advantage over traditional personals, because a lot of them are free and they have a wider reach. But this can also be a problem if you find someone interesting and they're in Alaska and you're in South Africa. It sure does intensify those first-date jitters when you have to fly halfway around the world to "go for coffee."

The great thing, however, is that you get to know someone before you see them. As with print ads or telepersonals, this should, theoretically, give the less-than-beautiful among us a better chance by avoiding appearance-based first impressions. Sadly, though, deep people that we are, no matter how well you get to know someone first, no matter how elegant their e-mail, one look and it can still be all over.

Sarah, a 27-year-old student living in Montreal, had a year-long e-mail relationship with a guy in Texas. They thought they were crazy about each other. He finally came to meet her and, as soon as she laid eyes on him, her heart sank. She was not physically attracted to him at all.

On the other hand, I know a woman in Montreal who just married a guy from Montana she met on the Net.

Even though the Internet makes the world a Global Village, sometimes you fall in love with the boy next door — quite literally. "I was chatting with a guy on-line for a long time," writes Margaret from Winnipeg, "and then we finally realized we only lived five blocks from one another."

Like joining clubs or taking classes, the Net can put you in touch with people with similar interests through special-interest forums on every subject from airplanes to zoology. It's a little less blatant than cruising the newsprint personals, and it gives you something to talk about.

There are also commercial web sites for people looking for a date: www. datecentral.com and www.couple-link.com are just two examples. An electronic combination of a "relationship consultant" and a personal ad, these sites allow you to peruse personality profiles and photos to find a partner. Many also offer dating and relationship advice, along with some other bells and whistles.

# Cruising Tips

Some things to consider if you're cruising on-line:

- Given the volume on the Internet, it's even more important than it is with regular personals to make yourself stand out from the crowd. Details, details… "Hi, I'd like to meet someone…Please write!" ain't gonna cut it. While you're at it, try not to sound too pathetic or desperate. And don't think that if you write a really explicitly sexual ad, you're gonna nab yourself a cyber one-night stand. Especially if you're a woman. More likely, you'll just attract perverts.

- Women post fewer ads, but when they do post they usually get more responses. Men post more ads and get fewer responses, unless they're gay. It's the nature of the beast. So straight guys, be patient, and straight women, be picky.

- A warning to the guys: don't expect to post your ad once and then sit back and wait for the dates to roll in. Try posting it in different places every few weeks, and tweak it once in a while. See what works and what doesn't. That's the beauty of the Internet: you can alter your ad when you want.

- Remember that people can fake identities, even gender, on-line. You never know if that hot young babe you've developed a thing for isn't really a football jock.

- Keep your expectations in check. If you do develop a relationship with someone on-line, remember that the reality may be very different than the fantasy you build up. You may have a great e-mail relationship, you may get along great on the phone (if it gets that far), but you won't know if it's right until you meet the person.

- Then again, don't be too harsh if and when you do meet the person and things don't click immediately. Remember, you've been having a relationship with this person's on-line personality. It may be different than their real-life persona, but it's still in there somewhere.

- A final note of caution: there is plenty of weirdo potential here. Don't give out your address and phone number, and get a photo — it's not shallow, it's realistic. Get references from the person if you're uncertain, then do a background check. Hey, I'm perfectly serious. And again, if and when you do meet, make it in a public place.

## Do-It-Yourself Dating Services

If you don't like the available services, you can always become creative. I read one story about four single guys in Houston who pooled their money and leased a billboard for one month to display their personal ad. It cost $2,500, total, and they got more than 300 responses in 10 days.

As we hear all the time these days, you have to network. You have to put the word out that you're looking, just like when you're trying to find a job or an apartment. One woman I talked to, a copywriter named Melissa, got tired of waiting around for something to happen. At 34, she decided she wasn't going to find anyone who met her standards through the few dates that came her way.

"I was thinking there's probably only one percent of the population I'm going to get along with," says Melissa, "and if I'm only meeting three people every eight months, then what are the chances of me finding someone? It just felt like looking for a needle in a haystack." Melissa realized she needed "volume," as Rich Gosse would say (see "Single People Are Lazy!" page 49).

The personals were not a success. "I'd get calls from small-town dentists who just weren't compatible," Melissa continues. "It was just casting too wide a net, with no filtering process." And she didn't like the idea of a dating service (yes, the stigma). So, being a copywriter, she did what she was trained to do. She turned her search into a campaign: the Summer of Love Contest.

She contacted everyone she knew and created 19 teams of two to six members. "I teamed up people who I thought would have fun together. One group of friends was a team, my mom and my brother and his girlfriend were a team. The biggest team was a group of gay lawyers, because they seemed to know the least amount of straight men, so we lumped them together."

The campaign was launched on May 24, and each team was given until Labor Day to come up with one candidate for her to date. "There were no recruitment restrictions," she says. "I said to them, 'If you want to put an ad in the paper, if you want to interview men at Canadian Tire, I don't care.' I sent each of them a direct mailer telling them the rules, who was on their team and the prizes available to be won."

Well, yeah, there had to be some kind of incentive. "The prize for getting me out on a first date with their candidate was a free video rental of the romantic comedy of their choice for each team member. If I had a second date with a team's candidate, each team member would get a CD called *Retro Night Romance*. If I had sex with the guy, the prize would be a gift certificate from a sex shop, plus a bottle of Astroglide lubricant."

If Melissa and the date were to maintain a monogamous relationship for six months or more, the prize would be a flower arrangement. If the date resulted in co-habitation — no prize, but the winning team wouldn't have to help either of them move. And finally, if they got married, the grand prize would be dinner with the happy couple for all the teams and their dates at some fancy-schmancy supper club. Plus the winning team would get to tell the story at the wedding.

And yes, it's all at her expense. "I figure if someone finds me a husband, it'll be worth fifteen hundred bucks for dinner. Don't you think?" However, by mid-summer, not one candidate had materialized.

Melissa knew that, in any successful campaign, you have to keep up the momentum. So she sent out a newsletter, filled with info about "all of the hilarious things that people have been doing to find me a nice guy."

And how does it make her feel when, even with 19 teams at work, she still can't seem to get a date? "In a way, it's validating. Here I have 19 teams with up to six people on each, with all of their six degrees of separation, and they're all saying, 'We can't find anyone' or 'The guys we do find are assholes' or 'They're not good enough for you.' Well, either I'm the most perfect woman on the planet and no one can possibly live up to me, which is not true, or I'm thinking, 'Holy crap, it is as tough as I thought.'"

## Summer of Love Newsletter
## Vol. 1, July 16, 1998

When 34-year-old copywriter Melissa got frustrated because she wasn't meeting any good men, she did what she knew best: she created a campaign to find herself a date. Nineteen teams made up of friends and relatives took part in the Summer of Love Contest. Each team was to come up with a male candidate for Melissa by the end of the summer. Like any contest, there were prizes. To keep up the momentum throughout the campaign, Melissa sent out the *Summer of Love Newsletter:*

Okay, so now that you've finally picked all the little purple hearts out of your underwear (hey, I know some of you opened your newsletter on the toilet), it's time for an update.

No teams have entered a candidate yet, but I ran into a friend in the grocery store, and she told me she's splitting with her husband, so I could have him if I want.

Marybeth says she lives across the street from Mike Bullard's brother, which is great because comics have hardly any emotional baggage.

Speaking of comics, my brother does stand-up and has vetoed all the guys he knows on the grounds that they're all busy starring in *Bitter, Intelligent Men Who Drink Every Night and Earn Only $12,000 a Year*.

James and Kathryn want to go national with a plea on *Speaker's Corner* and/or a segment on Real Life Network. Smoke and mirrors if you ask me, but cameramen are often cool and cute.

Wendy wants to set me up with her city councilor. Good, I'll hassle him about the lame-ass antismoking by-laws.

Leah says she has a really good candidate, but he's 50. Sorry, Leah, team members are not allowed to submit their fathers.

Armando wants to set me up with his friend who's 25. Okay, people, there are some points for how long your candidate can sustain an erection, but even more points for how long they can sustain a conversation.

My sister says she knows guys from the Owen Sound bus terminal...

My aunt and uncle say they're just going to go to the pub and grab someone who looks right. Heck, I've done that.

Daphne hasn't quite grasped the concept that they must be single, but that's okay because she's submitting musicians.

Catherine and Ian have actually initiated a photo swap with an engineer who races motorcycles. Excellent work!

And Mark, Marc, Daniel, Rob and Dave are using the lame excuse that because they're gay, they don't know anyone. Actually, if they did find a nice, funny, cute, sensitive, single, politically conscious, feminist-identified, non-homophobic, self-aware guy, we'd all assume he was in the closet anyway.

As you can see, it's still pathetically wide open. So, there is now a speed prize — a $100 tab on me at the bar of your choice — to be awarded to the first team that puts forth a valid candidate in a mutually agreed upon social setting.

Of course, all I'm really looking for is someone who's kind of funny and maybe has a dog and a motorcycle. And if they play bass, bonus! NOW GET OUT THERE AND SCOPE SOME POONTANG!

## No Delivery Service

There are a lot of things you can do to try to bring two single people together, especially if they're willing to pay for it. You can get them to come up with a shopping list of likes and dislikes, get them to buy ads to describe themselves, even get them to exchange photos. But no service can arrange that all-important spark, and we all know that if the spark ain't there, most people won't give a relationship much of a chance.

Remember, dating services are not in business out of a genuine concern for your loneliness. Plenty of services are free to women because that's the only way they can get them to join. While that's great for women who want to try these services, let's not forget that they're free in the first place because not too many of us have much faith in them.

I know people are struggling out there, and our busy, stressful lives make it hard to meet people, but I can't help but think these types of services are only making matters worse. They make being single seem like the plague, and they offer snake oil as a cure, cashing in on people's loneliness and our desperate belief that the only way we can be absolutely happy is as a pair.

There is no magic place or way to meet someone. What works for one person doesn't necessarily work for someone else. The main thing is that you gotta be out there and open to it. This is a biggie. You're not going to meet someone if you're not open or ready to meet someone. People pick up on this. They can sense back-off vibes a mile away.

You just gotta get out there. Yeah, it's tough. Sometimes it's hard to get over the fact that you're doing something specifically to try to meet someone. It has a certain smell of desperation about it. (That darn stigma again.)

But as much as it'd be nice if there was a delivery service for this type of thing, like I said in the beginning, you just ain't gonna meet many people from the comfort of your own couch.

# Single People Are Lazy!

Rich Gosse, the president of American Singles, has written several books on how not to be single. When I spoke to Gosse over the phone from his home in L.A., he didn't mince words. Basically, he says, single people don't meet anyone because they're picky, they're lazy and they're liars. Better let him explain:

J: What's the best way for people to meet these days?

R: The number-one way is through personal ads. That's the easiest, most efficient way to go through thousands of people.

J: A lot of people I talk to don't like them, partly because they feel people misrepresent themselves.

R: Well, of course they do. This is a nation of liars. I have a cynical attitude because I've been doing this for 20 years, and I've heard all the excuses that people have for not doing anything to meet people, all the whining and complaining and the fears. Personal ads are one of the safest ways to meet people. I tell people it's safer to meet someone through a personal ad than it is to meet them in church.

J: Why?

R: The guy next to you at church could be a hatchet murderer. I mean, hatchet murderers go to church. Just because you meet them at church doesn't mean you're safe. You're a lot safer meeting them through a newspaper, because before they run your personal ad, the paper gets your name, your address and your telephone number. Not too many murderers like to give that information to the news media.

J: It's still a bit of a lottery. When I go through the personal ads, there's not very much to distinguish one ad from another.

R: It's hard work. You have to play the numbers game. That's my whole philosophy: if you're a picky person, you have to go through a vast number of people before you find the one person who has everything on your list and you have everything on their list. In short, people who are not married are, by definition, people who are picky. And they cannot afford the luxury of waiting for Mr. or Ms. Wonderful to fall through the skylight.

J: How can American Singles help?

R: The first reason people join American Singles is because it's free, and single people are cheap. So the reason we're the world's largest non-profit singles organization is because we don't charge anything. We also have the world's largest web site for single people (www.cupidnet.com). We get a million hits a day. Through that web site, you can access a thousand different web sites just for single people. Whatever it is you're looking for as a single person, we have it on one of these web sites. On our home page, we have a calendar of singles events. We have over 1,000 events a month for singles all over the U.S., and we're starting to list events in Canada as well.

J: How do you shake the stigma of going to singles events? People are really hesitant. It makes them feel like they're…

R: Like they're desperate losers. The first thing I tell people is that I never have desperate losers coming to my events. Anybody who's desperate to be in a relationship, people who cannot bear to be alone, they never come to my events. I mean, there are millions of desperate people who believe that anybody is better than nobody. And we have a name for them. They're called married people. Now, a person who is single is obviously not a person who is desperately lonely, because if they were desperately lonely they would get involved with the first person who comes along who's willing to hang out with them.

J: That's a slightly more optimistic view of single people.

R: Right. The only people who come to my singles events, and the only people who join my organization, are people who are picky. But here's the bad news: picky people tend to be attracted to picky people. In other words, the longer your list is, the longer their list is. So, for example, let's say you're picky and only one out of 100 people out there is worthy of you. Let's say you interview them and you only want to date one out of these 100 people. Well, guess what? That person is just as picky as you are. What are the odds you're gonna have everything that is on their list? Probably not too great. They're probably gonna reject you. So you have to go out and interview another 100 people. The more picky you are, the more you have to play the numbers game. That's why I recommend the personal ads. They're the most efficient way to go through thousands of people to find the one person who works for you.

# Strange Encounters: You Met Where?

Where was your most memorable encounter?

"At a wrestling tournament."

"At a strawberry festival in Manitoba."

"At a music festival. The guy in the car next to mine was listening to a band I loved. I asked him to turn it up. We've been friends for two years now."

"In the Vatican! He was like 18 years old with shoulder-length blond hair, like a floppy-puppy-type guy. Very cute. I was, like, 23. The difference wasn't that big but it was to me. He followed me a bit and talked to me. He could barely speak English and I could barely speak Italian, and we ended up going out. It was really fun. We drove around on this really old motorcycle. He was so poor, it was unbelievable. We had to use our feet to pull the bike up hills. It was great."

"A coffee shop. Of course, I suppose the only thing that was strange was that I was drunk beyond comprehension, she was sober (she had to be, she was the counter girl) and I still got laid (albeit two months later). It ended up not being worth any of the trouble. Not to say I went to any."

"I went out with a woman I met at an intersection when we were both waiting for lights to change. We started talking and then went out for coffee. We went out for six months."

"A bagel shop. My friend would go get bagels everyday because she was in love with the guy behind the counter – we called him Bagel Boy. She devised this plan whereby she would go in and pretend she lost her sunglasses and ask B.B. if he'd seen them. Of course he hadn't, so she told him she really wanted them back because she got them in New York and could he please call her if anyone found them. She left him her phone number. She'd go in once a week, and one day she asked him to help her move some boxes or something. Then, to thank him, she asked him out for coffee, and he sort of shuffled his feet and said he was in a relationship. But they did finally go for coffee and ended up having this torrid summer romance. They're still seeing each other!"

"In a class. A mutual friend introduced us. It was during the Quebec referendum, so we had a referendum chat." (It's nice to know the referendum brought two people together!)

"At school. I used to run into him in the school office a lot. One day we decided to have coffee. We were in the cafeteria, and I went to get a muffin. It was the wrong muffin, and I didn't like it. The next week he baked me a muffin and brought it to school. I thought, 'Wow. He's very cool.'"

"At a coffee bar. It wasn't really a date, but at one point I realized I was drinking black coffee, and I don't like black coffee. That's when I began to think, 'Hmm...I like this guy.'"

# Movin' In for the Kill

## Are You Giving Me the Eye
## or Is My Fly Undone?

Okay, so you're in your feng shui class and you've got your eye on the guy with the best angles in the room. Now what do you do?

If it's not your fear of rejection that prevents you from taking action, then it's your uncertainty about whether this person gives a flying cahooney about you, right?

Sometimes it's hard to know if the person is smiling at you from across the room or smirking because your fly's undone. Sometimes you're too dense to realize that running into the same woman every morning when you get your coffee is more than a "coincidence" on her part. Sometimes you read into things too much and imagine that running into the same woman every morning when you get your coffee is not a "coincidence" on her part.

Add to all this the delicate issue of trying to suss out someone's availability, and you've got a lot of people going home alone.

"I am so bad at approaching people," says Yves, a 31-year-old gay video-store manager. "Ally McBeal has nothing on how neurotic and dumb I can be."

Well, kids, here's the bottom line: if someone's interested and available, you could shoot spitballs at them and they'd find it charming. It's the ones who haven't yet realized that you are the one who will make their life complete who are more of a challenge. Or the ones who you'd like to maybe just take for a test drive. You've got to find a way to make them come over to your side.

And it's all in the approach. One false move and you could blow it.

Whether you're a man or a woman, straight or gay, putting the moves on someone is tricky business. It's all fun and games until someone throws you a bad pick-up line or moves in way too fast. And even if you get his or her attention, how do you know they're really interested? More on all that in a bit.

But first, just in case you thought we're the only ones who have to go through this hell, a little history.

## The Historical Approach

As the old story goes, back in Napoleon's day, a certain Prince Regent made a rather valiant attempt to get this babe, a widow named Mrs. Fitzherbert, to go out with him. According to E. S. Turner's *A History of Courting,* the prince "beat his brow, popped his eyes, tore out his hair and writhed on the floor. He threatened to carry her off to America by force; he drank three pints of brandy and, finally, in a last-ditch attempt to woo her, sent her a message saying he had stabbed himself. She went to his bedside, fainted at the sight of blood (which some believe he had faked) and then skipped town."

They did eventually marry, but it didn't last. There is such a thing as trying too hard.

Then again, there was also a time back in 17th-century England when guys were fined and imprisoned for pursuing women at all. It was strictly her father's responsibility to find her a husband, end of story. Unapproved candidates need not apply. I suppose that would be one way to avoid the stress of trying to find a date.

When you look back in history, it's not hard to understand why guys today are a little confused about how to approach a woman.

For example, in 18th-century England, courting a woman was more about getting laid than about love and marriage. Guys went all out trying to win that special lady's heart. Again, to quote *A History of Courting*: "[Serenading] had achieved special notoriety in Nottingham, where young ladies complained of riotous lovers infesting the streets with violins and bass viols, from midnight to four in the morning."

Talk about overkill.

But things really got out of hand when the Romantics raised amorous expectations with all their "still hearts" and mushy poetry. The Romantics set a dangerous precedent, writes Turner, because women were "stuffing their heads with romantic nonsense." What's a romantically challenged love-struck boy to do? Why, hire a romantic, *à la* Cyrano de Bergerac, of course. (If you saw the movie *Roxanne*, with Steve Martin, you'll know the story.)

Today, women still want to be serenaded. However, hardly anyone plays the lute anymore. And now, *Cosmo* magazine sets women's expectations when it comes to wooing. That means we women want men to romance us, except when we don't, and we also expect to be free to approach men.

Of course, without years of serenading practice or men's magazines telling us how to woo a man, girls have got even less to go on. And, truth be told, women hitting on guys is still a relatively new concept. Some of us (both men and women) aren't completely comfortable with it yet.

But forget about history – most of us got our romantic education on the playground. If you liked someone, you chased him or her around the schoolyard and then gave 'em a good slug in the arm when you caught them. I still have a piece of pencil lead in my hand where a boy who liked me in Grade 5 jabbed me.

It didn't get much better in high school. There, if you really liked someone, you played it super-cool and ignored him. If you were really brave, you got your friend to tell him that you liked him. Then you ignored him.

Now that we're mature adults, and walking up to a person in a bar and slugging them in the arm might get us charged with assault, what are we supposed to do when we like someone?

## Death to the Pick-Up Line

You'd think pick-up lines would be a dead issue by now. They don't work. I don't know that they ever did. Who started that whole thing anyway? Guys, was that you? If there was ever a time when we led you to believe that these lines work, we're sorry. We were only humoring you because we felt bad that you had to do all the work.

I know it's tempting to try to come up with something clever to say so that you stand out from the rest, get to display your particular charms and start the ball rolling. But honestly, walking up to a woman, sticking out your tongue and saying, "If I buy you a drink, will you sit on this?" is just not an appropriate way to introduce yourself. (Yes, someone actually did this.) The thing is, if someone isn't interested, you're wasting your time and your clever (or not-so-clever) line.

So if you find yourself searching for a good opening line, stop yourself right there. She can tell you've been working on it. I'm sorry to harp on the guys about this, but it does seem to be mostly a guy thing. Like I said before, I'm sure that has something to do with the amount of pressure on you to make the first move. But honestly, most people (men and women) would rather hear a genuinely delivered "Hi there" than a comedy routine. "The most effective lines are honest statements," as Karen put it.

In fact, most of you said the most effective line is...wait for it: "Hi, my name is..." Variations on "Hello" can work, but they have to be sincere. Something along the lines of "Hey, I couldn't help but notice you dancing tonight. You look great. My name is..." certainly could be a winner.

But to a certain extent, what you say is fairly inconsequential. If there's a mutual attraction, most any opening statement (except for that idiotic tongue line) will do. "Your smile lights up this room" can melt you if you wanna do the person delivering this line, but it can sound like a big hunk of cheese if you don't.

If you want to pique someone's interest, and you don't feel a simple "Hello" is a strong enough self-marketing campaign, keep it simple. Don't try to be too clever. Compliments work well – if they're genuine and don't involve certain body parts. "You're great to talk to" rather than "You have nice tits," for example. But don't get carried away. Too many compliments of any kind and you start to sound insincere.

"An appeal to my intellect – that always works," says Jennifer. "'Hi, what book are you reading? It looks interesting,' for example." Mutual interests provide a good opening. "Oh yeah, I love that painting too," if you're at the art gallery, let's say. This gives you something to talk about.

On the other hand, "You're so beautiful" doesn't exactly open the floor up to conversation. Whaddya supposed to say? "Oh, you really think so? I think I'm pretty damn hot myself."

Any "So do you come here often?" type lines are out, out, out. Again, though, if you suss out whether there is interest first and then phrase it genuinely, something along the lines of "It's my first time here, how 'bout you?" could work. Or "I've noticed you before. I really like coming here because…" might stand a chance.

"I like someone who will reveal information about himself before asking for information about me," says Sarah. "That way, it's an exchange, and it's not about, 'I want information. Give it to me.'"

## That Was the Worst Line I've Ever Heard

According to *A History of Courting*, back in the fifties in Communist Burma, lines like, "You are beautiful," were not only cheesy but were also considered hopelessly bourgeois. A hot line back then was often politically oriented and went something like: "I am deeply impressed by your qualities as a faithful and energetic member of the Party, and I wish to wage the Party struggle together with you."

Try *that* in a bar sometime. Although, it seems that people in the free world do fine coming up with some pretty odd lines on their own. Consider these examples from two of the people I spoke to: "I wish I were that coffee machine over there so I wouldn't feel sad if you were to walk away from me." And, "You are a Canadian savings bond I'm interested in investing my time in."

Some of the worst one-liners collected go from the poetic – "Hey mother, want another?" – to the ridiculous – "Your eyes are so beautiful. I could fall in love with you." (This latter gem comes courtesy of Tara, a free-spirited 29-year-old who says some guy came out with this "five minutes after he met me.")

Then there's the just plain cheesy: "Can I look at the tag in your shirt to see if it says 'Made in Heaven'?"

Lines delivered purely in anticipation of sex are always, um, interesting. "Nice shoes. Wanna fuck?" is one Martin's gotten some use out of, believe it or not. It has a certain appeal if, well, if it's obvious you want to fuck the person. "It gets their attention anyway," he says.

But this kind of direct approach can be a little unsettling. "I was in Toronto, having a drink at a gay bar, and some guy came up to me – he was quite good looking – and said, 'You wanna fuck?'" says Sam. "I couldn't believe it. I was dumbfounded. I said, 'I'm Sam. Who are you?' Later, I had a good laugh about it."

It makes ya wonder: these lines must work if folks (see guys, I'm lettin' you off the hook a little there) keep dishing 'em out like this. Well, according to Sam, sometimes, if he's horny enough, they do: "I went to the bar with a raging hard-on and had a bit to drink, and someone came on to me with some sleazy line, and I was like, 'Okay, you're breathing? Let's go.'"

Sleazy lines delivered on a bet, on the other hand, are not so welcome: "My face is leaving in five minutes. You better be on it." Robert confesses he delivered that one on a dare from his buddies. "Ach! The woman almost slapped me, but I got a big laugh from the guys." We'll bet you did – but was it worth it?

And finally, adding gimmicks only makes a bad line worse. "One of the first times I ever went into a gay bar was in Alberta," says Sam. "A guy came up to me in a cowboy hat lit up with Christmas lights and delivered the 'Do you come here often?' line. Was I impressed? Not really."

Like I said, death to the pick-up line.

# Snappy Comebacks

The one thing really bad lines are good for are snappy comebacks. Next time some-one tosses a stinker your way, instead of kicking yourself half an hour later and thinking, "Damn, I should have said…," try one of these clever rebuttals:

Bad Line: "Haven't I seen you someplace before?
Snappy Comeback: "Yeah, that's why I don't go there anymore."

BL: "Is this seat empty?"
SC: "Yes, and this one will also be if you sit down."

BL: "So, wanna go back to my place?"
SC: "Well, I don't know. Will two people fit under a rock?"

BL: "Your place or mine?"
SC: "Both. You go to yours and I'll go to mine."

BL: "I'd like to call you. What's your number?"
SC: "It's in the phone book."
Response: "But I don't know your name."
SC: "That's in the phone book too."

BL: "I'm here to fulfill your every sexual fantasy."
SC: "You mean you've got both a donkey and a Great Dane?"

BL: "If I could see you naked, I'd die happy."
SC: "Yeah, but if I saw you naked, I'd probably die laughing."

BL: "Hey cutie, how 'bout you and me hitting the hot spots?"
SC: "Sorry, I don't date outside my species."

BL: "I would go to the end of the world for you."
SC: "Yes, but would you stay there?"

*For straight girls only:*
Man: "So, what do you do for a living?"
Woman: "I'm a female impersonator."

Man: "Hey, come on, we're both here at this bar for the same reason."
Woman: "Yeah! Let's pick up some chicks!"

# Dance with Me:
# Choreographing Your Approach

Anthropologists and biologists with way too much time on their hands have spent hours in bars studying human mating behavior. Thanks to their efforts, they've discovered that we humans have a whole dance number programmed into our genes for when two people are checking each other out. Apparently, we go through a series of well-choreographed moves. You leer at her, she leers at you. She smiles coyly, maybe plays with her hair. He runs back to his table like a scared rabbit.

Yeah, I'm kidding. But you get my drift. Basically you tiptoe around each other until one of you moves in for the kill.

In order to get the moves right, let's take it step by step.

## 1. I've Got My Eye on You

"They can copulate with their eyes," I once read somewhere. Yup, there's no denying the power of eye contact. If you've ever held someone's gaze for that brief second longer than usual, you know what I mean. It's often what gets everything going.

Just be careful. "I have literally been checking someone out, trying to make eye contact, and walked into a wall," says Sarah.

Don't kid yourself. It's not just fear of walking into walls that makes it hard to look directly at someone you fancy and hold it for that extra second.

"At gay bars, I make eye contact and then look away. I'm so bad at it," says Yves. "Same goes for the 'eye contact on the street' rule."

Hang on a sec. What's this rule?

"Well, if you're walking down the street and someone makes eye contact with you, and you think you're being cruised, you just wait three seconds, then turn around, look back and see if he's still looking. But then what do you do? Because, at this point, you're like six paces apart, and unless one of you decides to run back, you've lost it! I usually just never look back because it makes me too nervous."

## Date from Hell

I'd moved into a new apartment and I didn't have any blinds for it yet, so I temporarily draped my terry-cloth bathrobe over my bedroom window. One night I was lying in bed (naked) reading a book, and I suddenly felt someone looking at me. I looked up and realized that the bathrobe had shifted, and I saw someone's silhouette quickly move away from the window. I managed to put some clothes on, get a butcher knife from the kitchen and tape the bathrobe up to cover the entire window. A couple of days later I was on my way home, and as I was crossing the street someone yelled, "Hey, you!" I turned around and there was this super great-looking guy in a great car, motioning for me to come over. As it turned out, it was the guy who had been looking in my window! Anyway, he apologized for scaring me and asked me out to a movie. Long story short, the guy was a major geek! A serious waste of a wonderful physique! That date was our last. I haven't seen him since, thank goodness.

Sometimes, it's hard to tell if the person is really looking at you. "Is he looking at me? I think he's looking at me. I'd better look at his eyes again and make sure he's really looking at me. Yes, he's really looking at me!"

But of course, since you're both so cool (read: terrified) about making eye contact, you both have an expression on your face that implies that the other person just shot your dog – which doesn't really signal "I'm interested."

This would be a good time to smile.

## II. Give Us a Smile

Eye contact followed by a smile can really do the trick. And we're not talking about a big grinning-idiot smile. Just a quick little George Clooney flash of teeth, delivered genuinely with a direct look at the person, and you're bound to make an impact if there's any spark of interest on the other end.

Of course, if you smile and the other person sticks out their tongue, it probably means you should move on (unless you're still in elementary school).

At this point, as far as I'm concerned, there is no need to get your tongue involved in the action at all. Some experts (see "When All Else Fails…," page 77) suggest that women put on lipstick and then lick their lips while the guy is watching. Yeah, that should be good for a laugh. At least he'd be smiling. Call me conservative, but I'd go for a slightly more subtle approach. Same for you guys. No lipstick.

## III. Word Play

You exchange a few glances and a smile or two – and you're certain it's not because you have food on your face. You finally get up the courage to walk over and say, "Hi." That's right, no cheesy line, just "Hi." Then you stand there like an idiot, completely stumped about what to say next. "Uh, terrible cold snap, huh?"

It's a problem. According to *A History of Courting*, even in the days of the Renaissance, when the fashionable lover was expected to "weep seas, live in fire, eat rocks, tame tigers," it was most important that "he have the gift of the gab."

Being able to strike up a good conversation is way up there on the lists of both men and women when it comes to the best way to win them over. And that does not mean you must become marathon mouth. The key to a good conversation is to express genuine interest and curiosity. Always be aware of how long you've been talking and how long ago you asked a question.

"I was with a group of women at this bar, and all of us were pretty hot for this one guy who was there," says Dawn. "We finally got him to come over and sit with us, and I ended up going home with him. He told me the reason he liked me was because I asked him questions about himself.

"I thought to myself, 'Why can't men figure that out?' If you're going to give men a tip on meeting women, it should be to ask her about herself."

Hear that, guys? Just don't turn it into a cross-examination.

"If you're asking all the questions of the other person, it's not fair," says Nathan. "You have to give enough information about yourself so that the other person feels a balance and finds out something about you too."

But not too much information. "I was at a movie and this guy kind of latched onto me," says Jennifer. "Within minutes, it seemed, he started telling me about his ex-wife, and how he is a romantic, and how awful it was being alone on Valentine's Day, but how he's not ready for a relationship. Needless to say, I cooled to him."

Easy, eh? Really, though, it can be fun. In fact, turning it into a game can spark some excitement. "Word play is a big turn-on," says Mark. "I love it when I can play with someone intellectually, and not in a restrictive or stuffy 'let's show off how smart I am' way, but with good intellectual banter. I like that."

"I say something fucking inane like, 'You know that "trumpet" and "tri-umphant" are from the same root?'" says Walter, a 28-year-old engineer and obvious wordmaster. "If they think that's intriguing, I know I've got a good thing."

Finally, don't get too panicked about a few moments of silence. You don't have to fill every second with conversation. A pause here and there gives the other person a chance to take the lead or create an out if he or she wants one.

And it beats having to start talking about the weather!

## IV. You're Really Funny

Humor's next on the list. Most people like someone who can make them laugh.

"To me, humor implies intelligence," says Mark. So it's obvious that being able to talk out of your butthole *à la* Jim Carrey is not the kind of humor we're aiming for.

Many of the people I talked to said that someone who's witty and playful gets them every time. But you don't want a one-man or one-woman show. Just someone who doesn't take themselves and the world too seriously. Someone who also knows how to be funny without being mean or too crass.

You also want someone who appreciates your sense of humor.

"I like a guy's who's funny, but funny in a way that allows me to be funny also," says Ann-Marie. "If a guy thinks you're funny, it's a big deal. My girlfriends think I'm funny. Guys don't. The guy I'm seeing now won me over because he thought I was funny. I was like, 'Wow, this is great! I got a guy laughing.'"

If you think someone's funny, tell them. Saying to someone "You're really funny" is a great compliment, but only if you mean it. You don't want to encourage them if they're a talking butthole.

## V. Prop-er Behavior

Back in the old days, masks and fans were popular flirting props. They gave you something to hold, or something to drop and have someone else pick up for you, or something behind which to hide from that creep who kept trying to make eye contact. Fans even developed their own language. According to *A History of Courting,* a fan touched to the left cheek apparently meant, "I want to get rid of you." A fan touched to the lips said, "Kiss me."

You can't say "Kiss me!" with a smoke, but cigarettes are to flirting today what the fan was to bygone days. Smoking became part of flirting from the day it became socially acceptable for men and women. At the time, "Some theatergoers complained that the business of exchanging and lighting cigarettes constituted 90 percent of the new love-making," according to *A History of Courting.*

A cigarette can come in handy as a pretext for opening a conversation, or for covering up an awkward pause. Although, it's best if you already smoke. And these days, that's less and less likely.

Drinks are another handy prop. You can hold one, buy one for someone, maybe even have the waiter send one over. However, sending someone a drink can be risky. Plenty of people will accept a free drink even if they're not interested in you. They may just be broke. Best to ask first if you can buy them a drink. Then judge the response.

Dave Hingsburger is a sex therapist who works with developmentally disabled people. A while back at the annual sexuality conference in Guelph, Ontario (one of the biggest such events, which attracts people from around the world), he told a great story about buying someone drinks. He was in a bar with a friend of his – a woman with cerebral palsy.

"Have you ever been to a bar with someone in a wheelchair?" he asked. "People send you 'pity drinks.' This woman would talk about how it was patronizing, but she drank them anyway. She had that edge of hypocrisy that made her truly interesting.

"Anyway," he continued, "this guy in the bar was sending her a lot of beer, and she says, 'If he sends over another beer, I'm gonna go talk to him.' Of course the guy sent over another drink, and she went over and said, 'Listen, buster, one more beer and I expect to get laid.' The guy's mouth hit the table, and he was out of there."

I'll drink to that.


## VI. Touchy Subject

There's nothing like a well-timed brush of an arm or a gently placed hand on a shoulder to get sparks flying. Just make sure the person is open to it. Unwelcome touch is about the worst move you can make.

Where you touch someone is important too. "Knees are good. Backs are good. Asses are bad," says Alex, a 31-year-old retail clerk.

Again, it depends on how you feel about the person touching you. "If it's someone you really like, they could probably touch you anywhere and it would be okay," Alex continues. "If it's someone you don't like, and they slide their hand across your back — eeew!"

Best to reserve touching for the more advanced stages of an encounter, when you're pretty sure you're in. If you must, keep it to a gentle touch of the shoulder or elbow to emphasize the intelligent remark you just made. Or a gentle, friendly jab in the arm (not like in grade school) if they say something particularly clever or funny.

It the person tightens up or cringes when you touch them, that's it, hands off!


## The Gentle Art of Flirting: Avoiding the "Drunk Uncle" Approach

In flirting, Rule No. 1 is *don't try*. The danger with trying is that it's one step away from trying too hard. Flirting is — or at least it should be — a natural act.

"The key to being a good flirt is to flirt without intention," says Lise, who is very much a pro-flirter. "You don't have to have sex with the person *that night*."

Hmm, what a concept.

Rule No. 2 is keep it subtle. I tried to explain this to a male friend who couldn't figure out why his "Hey, Bra Girl!" salutation to a woman at a party didn't exactly win her over.

I know men are afraid they'll be perceived as macho assholes if they approach women. That's because women think men are macho assholes if they approach them in the wrong way. Then again, men are always saying they want women to be more sexually aggressive. So women start flinging themselves at men with all the subtlety of a freight train. We both lose.

Thus, Rule No. 3: no flinging. In fact, you should avoid body contact of any sort until flirting is well under way, and then keep it to the brush of an arm or the well-timed elbow touch. Of course — and I can't stress this enough — only after you've been given the go-ahead.

Which brings us to Rule No. 4: be perceptive. "You have to be able to read the leave-me-alone signals," offers one pro. A good flirt is an expert at reading body language and respecting personal-space zones. Just because you've managed to maintain eye contact across the room for that fraction of a second longer than usual doesn't mean you can move in for the kill. Don't get too close unless invited, and if things suddenly cool off, that is not a signal to try harder (see Rule No. 1).

Rule No. 5: be prepared to back off. Even if you thought things were going swimmingly, when it comes to flirting, either party reserves the right to stop the game at any time without explanation.

Rule No. 6: drinking and flirting can be hazardous. While a splash of alcohol may help grease your flirting gears, too much can turn you into a grease-ball and dull your ability to respect Rule No. 4. Any flirting that starts with "Have I ever told you…" or involves any sliding hand movements (you know very well what I mean) is out. This is not flirting, but pent-up sexual tension, and it ain't pretty.

The trick is to find a happy medium somewhere between Bra Man's tactic and the drunk-uncle-at-a-party approach.

## Flirting: The Good, the Bad and the Really Bad

Here's what the people I spoke to had to say about the art of flirting:

**What Makes a Good Flirt?**

- "Good delivery. Not too smarmy, not too cool."

- "Having a sense of humor about it."

- "Good timing."

- "Being perceptive enough to know when to turn it off."

- "Looking you in the eye."

- "Paying attention to someone – whether it's a subtle pat on a shoulder, a strategic brush of the arm or simply a confident, warm look in your eye."

- "Sincerity."

**What Makes a Bad Flirt?**

- "Lack of humor and a sense of desperation."

- "Being a bragging idiot."

- "Putting me on a pedestal. That's a turn-off for me."

- "Being a loud, groping drunk."

- "Not being able to read body language."

- "Focusing on my ethnicity. In this day and age, some people still don't get it. They'll say, 'You must be Chinese,' and I'll stare at them and say, 'You don't want to go there. Don't get me started.'"

## How to Pick Up Girls (if you're a boy)

Honest, it's not that women are playing hard to get or that we enjoy shooting you down when you try to pick us up (unless you deserve it, that is). Usually, we're just being cautious. Hey, a girl's gotta be a little picky. We don't want to end up going home with an ax-murderer or, even worse, a guy who wears white socks with sandals. You can never be too careful.

So just how do you tell whether a woman is interested in you?

Well, the most obvious sign is if she approaches you. Trust me, women won't initiate any kind of interaction with a guy unless she's curious in some way. That doesn't mean you should come running over if we smile at you. Be cool; you've got time. Let her watch you for a while. Catch her glance a few more times, just to be sure there's something going on.

Even then, there's no need to pounce. She's still just checking you out, and if you move in too fast, before she's decided she wants to pursue anything with you, she'll wiggle out of it even faster.

Guys may not realize this, but women scope out men just as much as men check out women, and chances are we've got you pegged before you even come near us. So consider how you're conducting yourself. The way you treat the people you're with reflects on you big time.

Try not to make it too obvious that you're cruising. She wants to feel like she's the only one you've got your eye on. Like you picked her because she's just so darned special.

No comments on her body on the first encounter, not of a sexual nature anyway. You can compliment her funky outfit maybe, but that doesn't mean you say, "Wow, that dress makes your breasts look great!"

Oh, by the way, just one of my pet peeves. I can't stand a guy whose idea of conversation is to tell you how much the place you're in sucks or how the people there are a bunch of losers. It's not witty; it's cynical and boring.

Consider that if a women does respond to you, it doesn't always mean she's interested. Some women are way too nice, and they'll talk to you only because their mama taught them not to be rude.

Let her take the lead, but don't sit back and let her do all the work. If she's uncomfortable, she'll let you know. Just make sure you're not so busy trying to charm her that you don't pick up on her discomfort.

Be alert. We love a guy who can pick up on our signals. Watch her body language and read her verbal and physical clues. If she steps back while you're talking, she's literally backing off. If she's looking around while you're talking to her, she's looking for an escape or a rescue team. If she starts telling you about how she's escaped from prison twice and killed her whole family, she's probably trying to not-so-subtly blow you off.

The idea is to be charming but not "a charmer." Here's Karen's take on the subject: "I like a guy who's confident and sure of himself without being cocky." If you've got a nice butt on top of it all, bonus.

You may think we're being bitchy if we give you the cold shoulder, but the problem is, sometimes guys just don't get the hint. No matter how blatant we are about our lack of interest, some guys take this as a sign to try harder. It isn't. Really.

## Signs That You're In with a Woman

So guys, how do you know she's into you?

- She compliments you.

- She laughs at your jokes.

- She hangs around and doesn't suddenly have to go to the bathroom.

- If she does have to go to the bathroom, she leaves her coat behind and asks you to watch her drink.

- She's genuinely engaged in the conversation and picks it up when there's a silence.

- She touches your arm/knee/shoulder.

- She doesn't flinch when you brush past her to grab an ashtray or pick up a drink.

- She's ignoring her friends.

# How to Pick Up Boys (if you're a girl)

"Show up at a bar in a short skirt."

"Breathe."

Okay, yes, I admit, as these responses from some of the guys I spoke to prove, when it comes to making the moves on a guy, women have a slight advantage. And perhaps because we've been at it less time, some of the tired moves guys make still work for us because it doesn't feel like a routine.

We can walk right up to guys and start talking, and most of them will respond. We can send you a drink, and it's a novelty, not a bad cliché. Ironically, the problem with approaching guys is that half the time they don't even clue in to the fact that you're coming on to them. Sometimes it seems as if, unless you walk up to a guy, pull your shirt up and say, "Me and my friends here would like to entertain you for the evening," the guy will almost always think you're making googly eyes at the fellow behind him.

"We choose to maintain our innocence," says Tom, a shy 30-year-old web designer, in defense.

"Yeah, we're just plain dumb," admits his more honest friend Michael, a 29-year-old who does something with computers (don't ask me to explain). "I've had women hit on me, and I'm sure they're just looking at me because I have snot in my nose."

"I'm actually not very aggressive in the hunting department," says Nathan. "So unless a woman makes it very clear that she wants to be with me, I probably won't respond. I'm not a big chaser, so I like women who make it easier."

And just how can women make it easier?

"She can come up to me!" Nathan offers.

"She can do anything!" adds Michael.

Oh brother, we're back on that, are we? Give us something to work with here, guys.

"Okay, bottom line. If a girl approaches you, she has to be able to talk," says Martin.

Sandy agrees, but adds, "It's probably based a little on the way she looks." This honest 18-year-old high school lad continues: "But if she's too good looking, I may be put off [read: intimidated]. Behavior is more important."

I am happy to report that while most of the guys I talked to said looks mattered, they also said a woman too concerned with her looks turns them off. As Tom put it, "If I find a woman is too concerned about her looks, I'm wondering, 'What are her priorities?'"

And even if she looks good, she has to have a sense of personal style. Guys seem to like that too. In other words, girls, it's not necessarily what you wear, but how you wear it. Or something like that. "I dunno…She has to project radiance," a somewhat confused Martin says.

Hmm…I can just imagine it. "My, look at that woman radiating at me over there. She must want to be with me." Anyway, before you girls throw your radiant, stylish selves at the first guy you fancy, some boys do have their limits.

"I don't like it when a woman presumes that I'm interested in her," says John. "Or that just the fact that she's interested in me is exciting to me." In other words, guys want women to play it cool too, until a mutual interest has been established.

What can I say? Women also get confused about what men want. Because, on the one hand, guys often say they'd love it if women took more initiative when it comes to making the first move, that it would take so much pressure off of them. But, on the other hand, we're still fighting that old negative stereotype of the "sexually aggressive woman." Everyone told us boys don't like "that type of girl."

Even some guys in their 20s, who should be over it, still buy into that. "I find it sort of repels me if a girl approaches me," says Sandy. So, much as guys say they want us to make the first move, I get the sense that they're not entirely at ease with it yet.

Of course, if you're the kind of girl who has no problem making the first move, you're probably not going to waste your time on these guys. As Ann-Marie says, "I like to decide what I want, then I go out and get it."

And sometimes that means you just gotta apply that old schoolyard approach. "I met this woman in a club," says George, a 31-year-old print shop clerk who goes to a lot of clubs. "I was dancing next to her, and then she bashed into me. It was this weird, aggressive flirtation. We started dancing together, being pretty rough, and then we started kissing, and she bit my tongue. It was weird. I was interested in this girl, but I had no idea what to do."

Safe to say, tongue biting, while no doubt intriguing, might not be such a good approach. But there are plenty of ways to put the moves on him without using your teeth. "Touching me while we're talking," is just one example Nathan offers. "It lets me know for sure you're interested."

And I imagine that exactly *where* she touches him shows him just how interested she is. Actually, I've often wondered what would happen if you just walked up to a guy you fancied and grabbed his crotch. I know if the reverse were to happen, the guy would get slugged, if not arrested. I don't know that a woman doing this would get the same kind of violent reaction. Kinda reflects the differences in how men and women approach each other, when you think about it.

## Signs That You're In with a Guy

How do you know you've got his full attention?

- He touches you.

- He's attentive.

- He asks you to save his spot while he goes to pee.

- He buys you a drink.

- He asks for your opinion.

- He includes you in conversations with his friends.

- He continues to dance with you after you bite his tongue.

## How to Pick Up Girls (if you're a girl) or Boys (if you're a boy)

Show up in a short skirt…Yes, I'm kidding.

Actually, you'd think gays and lesbians would have it easy when it comes to hitting on each other. They already have one thing in common – their gender – and they should know what works and what doesn't, based on first-hand experience.

Yeah, right. Gay people are just as complicated as straight people when it comes to cruising. And they come with their own set of rules. But since most of the people I talked to were straight, I hardly feel qualified to explain it all here. And besides, this is only a 200-page book.

Suffice it to say that I've had enough butch lesbians hit on me to realize they can be just as obnoxious as straight guys. Admittedly, it's somehow less obnoxious or threatening coming from someone who you know gets her period just like you do. Of course, lots of lesbians are perfect ladies when they approach another woman. They just show up at the bar with their U-Haul trailer and move in with the first woman who buys them a drink.

As for gay men, I can't say I've ever had any hit on me, so I'm not sure how obnoxious they can be. Some of the one-liners from gay men that I mentioned earlier seem to prove they can shell 'em out just like the straight boys. But I have been to plenty of gay bars and, frankly, I've always been a little jealous of the way gay men cut through all the crap. You catch each other's eye, you go home, you fuck (safely, of course). Beautiful.

Of course, you still have to figure out afterwards if you want to go out on a date with the guy.

## Sealing the Deal: How to Proceed Once You're In

Which brings us to that all-important moment: asking someone out on a date.

You've exchanged glances, had some good conversation and brushed arm hairs. Now one of you actually has to ask the other person out. This is the really scary bit.

"I was working with this woman and I thought she was really cool," Nathan recalls. "I was getting to know her a little bit better. She had a radio show and I'd listen to it, so we always had something to talk about. I finally asked her out, and she laughed at me. She said, 'Yer asking me out on a DATE?' She then reached down, pretended to masturbate and said, 'Why do I need you? I can do this myself.'"

Ouch! No wonder we're scared to actually ask someone out.

And the fact that it is so anxiety-provoking is probably why, in our eagerness to seal the deal, we blow it by moving too fast. You know, you meet someone, things have been going swimmingly, all the signs are there, you figure you're in — and you go for it. You invite them to your cousin's bar mitzvah right then and there.

Sometimes it's better not to push it right away. He or she might not be ready to move so quickly. As much as you feel like this could be your last chance on Earth to ask this person out, sometimes it's more effective to casually confirm your interest and say goodbye. This allows both parties to go off, reflect and make sure they are really interested. I know, it may give him or her time to decide they are not interested. But chances are they will appreciate the space and add it to their list of pros about you. It can also build a little anticipation.

Here's what you do. You simply and politely say, "It was nice meeting you. I'd love to talk to you again." Or, if you've been talking about a common interest — like, I don't know, cycling, let's say — suggest that maybe you should go cycling together sometime. Let him suggest how this might happen. If he's doing somersaults across the bar looking for a pen to write down his number for you, you know you're probably gonna see each other again.

A word on exchanging numbers. In this day and age, most women are hesitant to give out their number. Offer her your number, guys! It's better than having her make up a phone number. I know, I know, she never calls when you give her your number. There's a reason for this. Trust me, if she likes you, she'll call.

But some of us aren't so patient. "I don't like to do the whole phone-number exchange thing," says John. "I'll try to set something up right then and there, as opposed to saying, 'Let's call each other.' I just find that often amounts to nothing."

However, he admits that this strategy doesn't always get results either. "People are funny," John continues. "Even though they might be interested, women seem to want to say, 'Well, call me sometime and we'll talk about it.'"

Like I said, we like some time to consider things.

If you truly feel that you must set up a date on the spot, make it something casual. Again, no bar mitzvahs right off the bat. And don't be too insistent; it's a turn-off. No one should have to be convinced to go out with you. If you ask someone out and the person says, "No," that does not mean, "No, I will not go out with you that night, but perhaps another night."

A friend of mine said he would ask a girl out three times before he would give up. Hey, this is not baseball. Once is enough. If he or she really can't make it for the specific date you are proposing, they'll let you know. "I'd love to, but I can't. How about next week?" for example.

If she tells you how busy she is this weekend and adds, "But next weekend I'm totally free," that's your cue. If she says, "Actually, I'm busy every weekend for the next 10 years," it's probably a good idea to drop it.

If and when you do ask your prospect out, you might want to consider a weeknight as a first-date night. First of all, people often do already have plans for the weekend. Also, most of us are too busy to give up a precious weekend night for something that might turn out to be a dud. It also avoids giving the impression that you have nothing to do with your weekend and, by extension, that you have no life.

It also implies casual – that "Let's get together and do something sometime" feeling. No big deal. Just a chance to hang out. No pressure.

But by all means, if you're being asked out and are interested, don't hesitate. "I'd love to go out with you" is all it takes – and you're in.

## Who Asks Whom?

"Girls are always saying they want equal rights, but no way are they going to ask a guy out," complains Sean, a bitter 19-year-old dating veteran. "But then if you ask a girl out and she's not interested, you're a jerk."

Rough, eh? I know we like to think men and women are now equal in the "who asks whom" department, but quite honestly, I know we're still not – even in the big city. And if you're out in the boonies, where I'm originally from, or if you're from a more traditional cultural background, things are still very much "boy asks girl."

Like I said earlier, part of the problem is that some men still aren't entirely comfortable with a woman taking the lead. "Men will say they find it flattering if a woman approaches them," says 24-year-old Julia, a waitress who is speaking from experience. "But when it comes to the relationship stage, they say things like, 'This doesn't really count because you came on to me.' They find your assertiveness sexy at first, but then suddenly you're 'pushy' if you continue to take charge."

Maybe that's why, as Mark suggests, "Rather than come right out and ask you out on a date, women will ask you out in more casual and subtle terms, so it's not so obvious." Something along the lines of, say, "I'm going to this concert on Saturday, and I just happen to have this extra ticket, and every single one of my friends just happens to be out of town this weekend, so if you want to go, you're welcome to the ticket."

Or we become sneaky about it. Because some women still aren't completely comfortable coming right out and asking, and because we know guys aren't always cool with us doing the asking, we'll set everything up – but let him do the asking. "Oh, you're going to that concert? Really? Oooh, I *love* that band. Too bad I'll be stuck at home that day doing nothing because all my friends are out of town." Then, lo and behold, he invites us. She gets her date, but he gets to take credit for asking her out.

Apparently, this scenario happens quite a lot. According to Leil Lowndes, who gives seminars called "How to Make Someone Fall in Love with You" (see page 77), two-thirds of all marriages result from women having made the first move or gesture. However, even when the woman does act first, the man will usually say *he* did. In other words, even if she hits him over the head with a two-by-four and drags him out on a date by the short and curlies, he will take credit for picking her up. That's the male ego for ya.

## When All Else Fails...
## There's Always that Old "Sticky Eyes" Routine

There are about 40 of us crammed into a room at a downtown Toronto hotel. We're at a seminar called "How to Make Someone Fall in Love with You," hosted by Leil Lowndes, author of the bestselling book of the same name.

"There are three cheap tricks to make someone fall in love with you – to make the spark happen – and they all happen with that first impression," she tells us.

Forty sets of ears prick up in anticipation. "Please, tell me the secret," their expressions scream.

For men, Lowndes announces, "Trick number one is 'sticky eyes.'" She says that women love to be looked at by a man she likes, so if you keep your eyes fixed on her, you'll get her phenylethylamine (the drug that pumps through our nervous system and bloodstream when we start to fall in love) flowing. If you really want to make an impression, our leader continues, give her the old "epoxy eyes," or "super-sticky eyes," if you prefer.

To do this, you're supposed to keep your eyes on her even when she's talking to someone else. So while she's turned to her friend to tell her about this creepy guy who won't stop gawking at her, you keep gawking at her to watch her reactions, to make her feel like you're really interested in her.

For the ladies, Lowndes recommends "the visual voyage." To perform this little number, let your eyes travel down his torso (no need to travel below the belt), then look him in the eye and give him a nod and a smile – the big seal of approval – and watch his chest inflate.

One participant wants to know if these techniques are guaranteed to work even for someone who's shy. Guaranteed! Is he serious? The bottom line, responds our host, is that "You can't make someone fall in love with you if they aren't attracted to you." Just a minor detail.

Next, she calls up a man who's confessed he fancies himself quite a pick-up artist (I suppose that's why he paid $40 to attend a seminar on how to pick someone up) and stages a pick-up. She tells him to choose a woman in the room he'd like to pick up. Big surprise, he selects the blondest, buxomest, biggest-lipped woman in the room. Then he walks right up to her and suavely asks, "You here by yourself?"

Oooh…big thumbs down there, buddy, tsk-tsks our host. Walking right up to someone and saying something usually isn't gonna work, she says. "It's how you approach, not what you say."

According to Lowndes, the sequence should go like this: First, catch her eye and smile. She'll look away, "because that's what women do." If she looks up within 45 seconds (apparently they've studied this), you're in. So smile again, and she'll look away again. Now you can approach her.

And what should the girls do to get him on board? She calls up one very brave woman to demonstrate. "Brush your hair back to expose your neck and look up at him through your batting eyelashes" is the instruction.

The woman actually does it. She's good, like she's auditioning for a bad porn video. It gets worse. Lowndes makes her practise the next seduction tactic: applying your lipstick and then licking your lips while the object of your affection looks on. "That's perverted," the woman protests. It was a little embarrassing.

Another technique Lowndes describes is the mirroring technique, where you do everything the person you're interested in does. This is how my brothers used to drive me crazy when I was young.

During the break, men are instructed to practise their sticky eyes and women to practise the visual voyage. Instead, most people have their eyes stuck on the extensive list of books and tapes Lowndes has for sale. The few who do meet and talk separate themselves into all-male and all-female groups.

My desire to flee before anyone gets their sticky eyes on me is overpowered by my desire to know why these people have paid 40 bucks each to pack themselves into a hotel room on a Friday night in order to learn how to lick their lips seductively. When I casually ask some of the guys whether they find it hard to meet women, they all say no. (Uh, right, guess that's why they're here.)

"It's meeting the right people and knowing what to do" that presents the problem, one guy says. And the brave lip-licker tells me she's there with a friend who wanted to come. Uh-huh.

Obviously, no one is about to announce, "I'm a loser who can't meet people and I have to come to a seminar to learn how to perform what is supposed to be a completely natural human act."

It's a little disheartening, somehow. They seem like such a nice bunch. So why are they having such a hard time? I can't help wondering if this stuff is actually helping. Having a person tell you that all you have to do to make someone fall in love with you is learn how to stare at them or eyeball their torso just right seems a little, I dunno, unfair. Did these people really think that these techniques would help? I imagine them venturing out into the world, sticky-eyeing perfect strangers or taking visual voyages down guys' chests, and feeling even more like losers because it still isn't getting them a date. That is, if they don't get slugged first.

# 4

# Details, Details

## You've Snagged a Date, So What's Next?

This is what constituted a first date in the Western world around 1900: Once a young woman had her first "season," as they liked to call it back then (her period for the slow ones out there), she was allowed to receive "callers" (guys who were hot for her). As we saw back in Chapter 1, a young man and young woman had to be formally introduced before he was allowed to come a-callin'. Since telepersonals didn't exist yet, this was usually done at church or some other community event. Once the two young 'uns were introduced, the young woman's mother might ask the young man to "call" upon her daughter. In some cases, if mom was feeling wild, she might let the young woman do the asking herself. "Calling" meant he'd come over and they'd sit in the parlor or on the front porch, or some such thing, and "get acquainted."

At least that's how the moneyed folk did it. In the lower classes, where people often lived in one-room homes, there wasn't really a way for a girl and boy to get to know each other without the whole family gawking on, so they – gasp! – went out in public. The rich saw what a blast the poor folk were having "dating" and wanted in on the fun.

Before you knew it, people were going to cabarets and dance halls on their first "dates." Then, by the twenties, moving pictures and cars caught on, and presto, picking up a gal and taking her to the movies became a classic first date.

When you think about it, this is where dating lost some of its quaint formality and women lost some control. Instead of a woman deciding to allow a man to call on her (when her parents gave the okay), and the two of them getting to know each other one-on-one in the privacy of her home, dating became a public event (the private back-seat boogie came a little later), which required money and maybe even a car. Guess who mostly had that stuff?

But I digress. At least in the past, whether it was at her house or in his car on the way to the movies, there was no mistaking a first date as a first date. Now half the time we don't even know what constitutes a first date.

If she invites you for lunch, is it a date? Is "Wanna go to a movie sometime?" an official first-date request? How about, "Let's go for coffee"?

And each of these first-date activities carries different significance. "Coffee" says "casual, anything could happen." A formal dinner date sets much higher expectations.

That's why, once you do get up the nerve to ask if maybe the other person just might, possibly, perhaps, by some wild stretch of the imagination, want to go out with you, that is, if they're not busy, what you do on this "sort of, maybe, kind of a date" is so significant.

The classics – a movie, coffee, dinner or drinks – all have their pros and cons. But there are lots of other things you can do on a first date, and you'll find some fun and slightly more unusual first-date suggestions in this chapter. Also included is a look at fashion: once you figure out where you want to go, *then* you get to figure out what to wear. And, finally, a major question: these days, who pays?

## Screening Dates

Once considered the classic first date, going to the movies has fallen somewhat out of favor as a first-date activity.

"The worst thing you can do on a first date is go to a movie," says Jordan, a 23-year-old commerce student. "Who wants to sit in the dark for two hours next to someone you don't know?"

"I dislike movies because you can't talk," echoes Caroline, a 29-year-old sports therapist. "You don't get to know each other." Caroline prefers football games or other spectator sports on a first date because you can talk, but you still have something to watch in the awkward moments.

Of course, not being able to talk at a movie can work in your favor if you're with a guy who doesn't know how to carry a conversation, Sarah points out.

Jennifer says she hates movies on a first date because "If you decide you don't like the guy, you've still got to sit through the whole movie, and you feel like an idiot."

But Tom says that's perfect. "If you don't like the guy, you can watch the movie and pretend he's not there. If you do like each other, you have something to talk about when you go out for coffee afterwards."

Personally, I hate first-date movies because I'm too self-conscious to get popcorn. And a movie just isn't the same without a big, greasy bag of popcorn to chow down on.

"Movies are great for flirting and building sexual tension," says Sarah's gay friend Megan, a 22-year-old travel agent. "Haven't you ever touched knees in a movie or put your arm around her seat and leaned in?"

That's cool on a second or third date, but not on a first date, says Sarah. I have to agree that a first-date movie is too soon to be making moves. You don't even know if you have the same taste in films yet. What if you find out later that, while you were tearing the film to shreds in your mind, she was thinking it was definitely Oscar material?

And it's not just as simple as "Let's go see a movie." When you see the movie also says a lot. A Saturday night is heavier than a Sunday night. Going to the matinee might not be taken as seriously as an evening movie. I find emerging from two hours in a dark theater into broad daylight kills the mood a little. Especially if it was a tear-jerker and your eyes are all bloodshot and your makeup's destroyed from crying.

Where you watch and what you watch are also laden with implications. "This guy asked me if I wanted to see his collection of *Get Smart* tapes," says Ann-Marie. "I thought that sounded kind of fun. But then he takes me to his place to watch them…and he lives in his parents' basement! It just didn't work for me."

I guess in the end a movie is an okay – if predictable – first date if you're not a big popcorn fan like me and you don't have to go into anyone's basement. But I prefer something even more casual for starters, especially if I'm not entirely sure whether I'm all that interested yet. In this case, I would say the coffee date is much more suitable.

## "Let's Do Coffee"

Actually, as Tom suggested, coffee after a movie (if you're on board with the movie date) is a nice combo. As Tom said, the movie gives you something to talk about. It can also be very revealing if one of you loved the movie and the other thinks it stank.

But a coffee date on its own is more of a "let me sniff your butt" date. "Let's go for coffee" is a non-committal, low-pressure way to chat and get to know each other. (You can decide afterwards if it was a date or not depending on how it went.) It's more like a pre-interview, a screening, if you will – an inexpensive way to meet someone, suss them out and decide if you want to go out on a "real date" with him or her.

It's a little awkward, however, if you don't drink coffee. "I never know what to do when people ask me to 'go for coffee,'" Nathan complains. "If I say I don't drink coffee, they think I'm blowing them off. And since I don't drink coffee, I don't feel right asking someone to go for coffee. But somehow, asking someone to go for a Dr. Pepper doesn't carry the same implication."

Personally, I think I'd be quite charmed if someone asked me to go for a Dr. Pepper. It's got that 1950s feel to it. And back then, going for a soda with someone was pretty serious stuff.

## Drink Up

Like going for coffee, going for a drink is another popular, casual, "not really a date unless we decide over this drink that we like each other" first-date activity. Having a drink together serves the great dual purpose of loosening things up and providing an opportunity to get to know each other one-on-one. Also, if things don't work out, at least there's a bar full of options.

But while getting pie-eyed together can be a great bonding experience, it can also impair your judgment. It's amazing what you can convince yourself of when you've wailed back six martinis in 15 minutes because you are so nervous. Him puking on your shoes may not seem so "cute" to you the next day when you're sober.

Which is why getting wasted together is not some people's idea of a good first date. "I agreed to go out with this guy, and he wanted to go to a pub on our first date," says Jennifer. "And I'm thinking, 'What? So you want to drink all night long?' Not the best first impression."

Going to a bar to hear some music at least gives going for drinks a purpose. "I like going to see a band," says Mark. "It gives you something to talk about, but it also gives you an excuse not to talk if you don't want to, because the music is so loud."

Seeing a band on a first date does force you to confront the other person's musical tastes right off the bat, which could be a good thing if they turn out to be similar to yours. If they're not, having to sit through a night of music you hate might be a little off-putting.

Drinks followed by or combined with dancing can be a lot of fun. If you've run out of things to say, dancing can be a great way to communicate and a great way to get physical without getting horizontal. Most women love a guy who's not afraid to dance. Just a word of warning, guys: if you still dance like you did in Grade 8, you might want to wait a few dates to go dancing, until we're smitten enough with you to be charmed by your "disco duck" moves.

## The Dinner Date

Let me just go on record here to say that I hate dinner on a first date. Even more than not being able to eat popcorn at a movie. There's enough pressure to keep the conversation flowing, so who needs to worry about whether you've got a piece of spinach stuck in your teeth while you're doing it?

Although, I do think watching someone eating for the first time can be very sexy (I said *can be*). I just don't want to necessarily do it myself unless I'm super-comfortable and we're somewhere casual enough that I don't have to worry about which fork to use.

Most of you agree that food on a first date is risky. "I don't like to go out for dinner because I'm a messy eater," says John. "I eat like a pig. I'm also a picky eater. I order weird things and then my date just thinks I'm a freak."

"I can't eat in front of a guy. It's not sexy," says Alison. "I just can't eat on a first date," echoes Carol. "No food on a first date!" is Yves's rule.

Another thing is that, unlike a movie, it's harder to ignore someone through dinner if you realize within the first five minutes that you're less than enamored.

If you still insist on dinner as a first date, consider that your choice of restaurant reflects on you. If you take someone to an upscale place and you're a downscale kinda person, your date may be charmed, but she or he also might think you're trying too hard to impress them. You also might have to foot the bill (more on who pays later), which can be an expensive drag if it doesn't work out.

Leil Lowndes, author of *How to Make Someone Fall in Love with You,* suggests that if someone offers to take you to dinner, it's a good idea to know a handful of reliable, not-too-expensive date restaurants where you know you'll be comfortable. (More on this later, but obviously it's less of an imposition if you go Dutch.)

### Date from Hell

I was on a date with someone and I was just getting over a cold. We were having dinner, and at one point I sneezed and a major booger hung from my schnozz for a second or two before I could blow it off. It was so embarrassing! She was good about it and didn't say much, although we didn't end up going out again.

Just don't suggest a place where you're going to run into a million people you know. It's a little obnoxious if your dinner is interrupted a thousand times by people coming over to say hello.

## Group Outings

My 18-year-old niece says she and her friends like to date in groups. It's certainly a low-pressure way to get to know someone you like and to watch them in action with other people. I'm just not so sure that it counts as a date.

My feeling is, for it to qualify as a real first date, the two of you have to go it alone. Besides, do you really want your friends there, snickering and pointing at the two of you from the corner of the room?

On the other hand, being with a group of strangers, like at a ball game or a concert, can be okay. But being with a group of strangers at a party on a first date is not. "The worst place I've been taken on a first date was to a party where I didn't know anyone but my date," complains Mark.

If you are planning a group-activity date, it's best to let the other person know.

"This woman I'd met only once offered to make me dinner," says Tony. "She also invited some friends but didn't tell me, and suddenly what I thought was a date turned out to be a dinner party with a bunch of people I didn't know."

Still, inviting someone you like to a dinner party can be a nice, informal way to get to know them a little better before asking them on a real one-on-one first date. Just make sure you let them in on who'll be there before they come over expecting dinner for two.

Whatever you do on a first date, my advice is to keep it informal. Your parents' house for dinner is not a good first-date invitation, for example. In fact, nothing involving family is allowed. The whole thing is nerve-wracking enough.

Save formal dates for later on, when you are more comfortable with each other. When you think about it, most of us do the opposite. We're all formal on our first dates and then, if a relationship develops, the dates become more and more casual. Until, eventually, ordering a pizza and renting a movie is considered a big date.

# First Dates That Rate

Here are some good first-date suggestions, courtesy of some of the people I spoke to:

- Going for a walk — but make sure it's scenic, so there's something to talk about. (And please, not one of those nostalgic tours of your childhood neighborhood — "That's the house where I felt a girl up for the first time…")

- An art gallery or museum, where there's something to talk about. (Unless you're someone like me, whose capacity for art criticism consists of statements such as, "I like it. It has pretty colors.")

- The theater. (This option can pose some of the same problems as a movie, but I like it because it's a little more unusual.)

- A comedy club. (Unless you quickly discover you don't share the same sense of humor, and she's yuckin' it up over some guy's fart jokes while you're crawling under the table.)

- Shooting pool, "because you get to see their bodies when they bend over." (On the other hand, one woman said the worst first date she ever had was with a guy who took her to a pool hall ["He knew I didn't like pool."] and then to a pizza joint ["I'd just told him that I didn't like pizza."])

- Cooking together, because "then you're at someone's house, creating some after-dinner activity potential." (Whoa there! Just remember, you might also be stuck at the person's house if you're not interested in any after-dinner activity.)

## And Now for Something Completely Different

According to *How to Make Someone Fall in Love with You,* it has been scientifically proven that the best kind of first date involves doing something exciting that gets that ol' phenylethylamine going (see page 77). At a seminar in Toronto, Leil Lowndes mentioned a study that was done in the U.S. in which a group of men was given either a mild or a strong electric shock. The men who received the strong shock were more attracted to the pictures of women that were shown to them afterwards. It seems there is something about danger and excitement that gets the sexual juices flowing.

In other words, if you want to get someone hot for you, shock them on your first date by doing something thrilling and unusual. Either that or bring a cattle prod.

Many of you agree that out-of-the-ordinary dates are the most memorable. "The dates I do remember are the ones where we did something physical and unusual," says Karen. "Somebody asking me to go rock climbing, for example. That kind of stuff, I just jump on. It's great because you can have fun together but you're not fixated on one another, you know, doing the Q & A thing."

"It's great to experience something different together," Caroline says. "It let's you see a person in a different context."

"That's why I ask people to an amusement park," says Mark. "There's plenty to do, so you can avoid awkward silences, but you still have a chance to get to know each other. And it brings out the kid in both of you." Could be fun – as long as you're not someone who tosses their cookies on rides!

Of course, some people are more open to unusual suggestions than others. "I remember asking someone to go bowling once and it was so out in left field for them, they didn't know how to respond," says Nathan. "They were like… 'Bowling? Sure, I guess. Bowling? Uh, why bowling?'"

In general, however, I think most of us are up for a challenge. "I'm dying to do something different. I can go to a bar or a movie – even out for dinner – any night of the week," says Jennifer. "If I'm going on a date, I'd like to go somewhere else."

I think so too. One of my more memorable dates was when this guy I had met called me and just said, "Be ready in half an hour." It was a beautiful summer day and he came by in a convertible, and we took off driving. He wouldn't tell me where we were going. We eventually went down this little dead-end road. He stopped the car, opened the trunk and pulled out all the fixings for a picnic, including a bottle of wine. We then climbed to the top of this cliff overlooking a lake and had a picnic. It was wonderfully exciting. How could I not be impressed?

Of course, the whole "unusual date" scenario can also make you realize how different you are. "Once a guy asked me to go birdwatching with him," says Alex. "He wanted to teach me about all the birds, and it was great fun – except it was six o'clock in the morning, and I'm not a morning person! And he did this every morning."

And sometimes you find out you're not as different as you thought. "This guy asked me to go to a boxing match," says Tara. "At first I thought, 'Obviously, this guy doesn't know me.' But then I was really curious and I actually found it really exciting." She ended up sleeping with him.

Odd dates can also reveal just how game the other person is. "I know this guy who took a woman to a wrestling match on their first date," Tara continues. "He figured if she could handle that, she could handle anything. They're married now."

## Think Positive

According to Lila Gruzen, co-author (along with Rebecca Sperber) of *10 Foolish Dating Mistakes That Men and Women Make and How to Avoid Them*, very few people have a really great first date.

"It's scary," says Gruzen over the phone from L.A. "You know, usually you really want it to work, you want to put your best foot forward. But most people are nervous and it really takes a special person to be at ease and be able to put their date at ease."

Gruzen's advice is straightforward: "Go out on your first date thinking about what an incredible person you are," she says. "How much you are 'enough,' how many areas you succeed in, how lucky people are to know you."

As opposed to what most of us do, which is to absolutely agonize about everything that's wrong with ourselves. By the time you're on the date, you're thinking, "Oooh, I know you probably don't like what I'm wearing, but…thanks for going out with me. How much do I have to pay you?"

## Fashion Statement:
## What You Wear Can Make or Break You

A friend of mine has this little game he likes to play when we're out. He tries to guess what number date a couple is on by what they're both wearing. "It must be their first date. He's got that 'I never wear these shoes and they're killing my feet' expression," he'll say to me, after sussing out a couple at a nearby table.

Whether in a job interview or on a date, clothes play a big role in the impression you make. Sorry, but it's true. Even Leil Lowndes agrees. Clothes matter, especially to women.

According to studies, Lowndes says, women choose men who dress better than average. As for men, it seems they don't really care what you wear as much as they care about the amount of skin you're revealing. In one study, men were shown pictures of women (dressed). The researchers found men to be most concerned with overall looks. They also noticed if she was wearing too much makeup. When it came to clothes, if the woman was showing a lot of cleavage, he'd say, "Hey, great dress."

The people I spoke to seemed to back these studies up. In general, women rated what men wore on a date as VERY important. "First impressions are lasting impressions," wrote Denise from Vancouver. And you thought men were the superficial ones!

Thankfully, most guys these days are pretty conscious about their presentation.

"At my high school, guys worry about how they look in front of girls," says 18-year-old Nadia. "They're like, 'Is my hair okay? Is my gel okay?' When you go near them, they're like, 'Don't touch my hair.' It's kinda funny."

"My brother will ask for my opinion about what he's wearing before he goes out," says Nadia's friend Amy. "The media doesn't just portray good-looking girls any more, they're also portraying good-looking guys. So there's pressure on them now too."

That's a good thing, she adds. "I want to feel proud when I walk down the street with my date. If I'm all dressed up, he should be too. I put effort into it, you know? I expect him to do the same."

Just in case you need some help there, guys, Nadia and Amy included a precise guide. "He should wear something casual, jeans or khakis, a sports shirt or a clean top (sweater, v-neck or rugby shirt)," says Nadia, who's obviously given this some thought.

"On the second date, he should wear something less casual, something dressier, like dress pants with a clean colored shirt. That way he shows he can be casual or dressy and can adjust to different situations."

You gotta appear flexible in today's market. Personally, my dress code is a little less strict. I like a guy with his own personal style, a guy who knows what works on him. Tom has found one way to nail this: "I have 'datable' clothes. You know, stuff that I know I look better in."

Many guys I spoke with seemed more concerned about women's comfort than what we actually wear. "Dress like yourself, be comfortable. Save the diamonds for a special occasion," says Nathan. "It should translate into a more comfortable date." Gee, thanks, Nathan.

That's not to say a guy doesn't like a little provocation. "I like it when I can see some skin," says honest John. "But not *too* sexy," adds Dimitri, a 27-year-old musician. As for me, I just try to wear something so I don't have to suck my stomach in all night.

Of course, it also depends on what you're doing on the date. Rock climbing in a little sequined strapless number, while no doubt fetching and unusual, may be a tad impractical.

"I always look at people's shoes," says Karen. "I think shoes say a lot about a guy."

So what are really bad shoes? "Anything really worn out. Like, a really scuzzy pair of 10-year-old running shoes really don't do it for me," she says. "Or shoes that don't match the rest of the outfit. Pointy Italian shoes don't work for me. Neither do loafers."

Which leaves…I dunno, flip-flops?

Obviously, dress is a matter of personal taste. But you want to be careful that you can keep up whatever appearance you first present. One day, many months down the road, your date could ask you, "How come you never wear that really nice Armani suit you wore on our first date, dear?" Are you gonna admit you borrowed the duds from a friend?

There are, however, some general style rules from my personal style file that I feel the need to share.

Guys: 1. No excessive (especially gold) jewelry and no open-necked shirts (especially if you've got a shag rug for a chest). 2. If you're going bald, wearing a baseball cap will not fool anyone. Some women say they find guys with ponytails sexy. I am not one of these women. But balding guys with ponytails are the worst. Just because you're going bald, you don't need to prove that you can still grow the hair you do have really long. No comb-overs either and no helmet hair – the eighties are over. 3. No sunglasses at night (especially indoors) and easy on the cell phones. The fact that you have one doesn't impress me, and the fact that you're using it while standing two feet from a pay phone is just plain stupid.

Women: 1. If you must wear the latest looks, don't wear them all at once. Can you say "fashion victim"? 2. No excessive hair products. When you move your head, your hair is supposed to move too. 3. Showing a little bra strap under your tank top is okay, but putting the entire thing on display is tacky. 4. Jogging pants are for jogging. 5. If you're gonna wear high heels, make sure you can walk in them. 6. As for sunglasses and cell phones, see point 3 under "Guys" above.

Of course, we all have our particular pet peeves when it comes to personal style (I get to vent mine because it's my book). But the one thing people were unanimous on is that, whatever you wear, *make sure it's clean*. I know it sounds obvious, but given the number of people who mentioned this to me, I'm beginning to wonder about the level of hygiene out there.

Speaking of which, don't neglect the undergarments. One never knows: what if you're in a car accident? Or even more scary, what if you have sex? As Miriam, a 31-year-old lesbian chartered accountant, put it, "You don't want to get caught with your 'period underwear' on and she takes off your panties and there's a big old stain and she happens to like having sex with the light on."

Or your underwear with the "pussy power" logo on them (although I found that story rather charming).

Getting dressed for a date is a great opportunity to get yourself revved up for the occasion. "I pump up the music and dance in front of the mirror," says Miriam. "I put on body lotion so I'm soft, some perfume so I smell good. I get my best 'date hair' going, gelled and tousled just enough to not look too perfect. If I think I'm going to have sex that night, I don't put rings on my middle finger. I totally primp, and then I walk out the door feeling like a million bucks."

Primped, primed and pumped is a good way to start a date. Just be careful how you pamper yourself. "I took a bath in baby oil before my date to make my skin nice and soft," says Jennifer. "But I leaned back and got my hair in it. This was back in the eighties when you wanted big hair, and I couldn't do anything with my hair. It was completely slick with oil and I had to wear it in this ugly ponytail. And then, during the date, I sat in gum."

Let's just hope she was a fabulous conversationalist.

# What Were You Thinking?

No doubt about it, clothing can really make a statement. Sometimes, however, that statement can leave your date speechless. Here are some of the worst things people told me they've had a date show up in:

- "A smelly sweater."

- "Nike sandals with gray work socks. YUCK!" (I'd just like to say that any sandals with socks are out. I would also like to mention that white socks are a particularly big no-no — unless you're wearing sneakers.)

- "A Hawaiian floral ensemble."

- "Pants that were way too tight, a shirt that he could barely breath in and unmatched socks. He was nervous and uncomfortable, and not just because of his clothes, although they didn't help."

- "Black shorts that made her already stubby legs look shorter and her behind look broader."

- "A leather vest. It looked awful and, besides, I'm a vegan, and I hate it when people wear leather."

- "A horrid dress. I didn't say anything, but I swear to God, it looked like someone had taken a paisley tea towel and fashioned it into a dress. It was BAD BAD BAD."

- "A pair of old jeans and a white T-shirt. We went to a nice Italian restaurant. The worst thing wasn't his outfit, but the fact that he didn't even take the time to shave. You kinda have to look good and smell good." (Basic hygiene people, c'mon!)

## These Days, Who Pays?

When dating moved out of the parlor (women's turf) and into the public domain (men's turf), not only was he now expected to do the asking, but because public activities like movies cost money – and, at the time, he was more likely to be the one with a job – he was now also expected to pay for the date.

Suddenly, dating was seen in part as a financial transaction. Guys were paying for female companionship. And some of them expected their money's worth. In fact, even today, exchanges of sexual favors for money, something we commonly refer to as prostitution, are sometimes called "dates." It's not hard to see where the "Hey, I bought you dinner, now you better put out" mentality came from.

As Beth L. Bailey writes in *From Front Porch to Back Seat,* "Men asked women out;…Men paid for everything, but often with the implication that women 'owed' sexual favors in return. The dating system required men always to assume control, and women to act as men's dependents."

If women lost some power in this new system, not all men were happy with it either. In *A History of Courting,* author E. S. Turner quotes one guy who wasn't too pleased with this economic model of courtship. He figured he had spent $20 a week for female companionship over five years, and he wasn't getting his money's worth: "I must say that the conversation, entertainment and mental companionship that I have received in return for this $1,000 a year seem to me to be priced beyond their real value."

All in all, it was an unbalanced system. Thankfully, now that most women earn their own living, we can share the expenses of dating – much more fair. As someone who usually goes out with artist types – i.e., men with no money – I usually share expenses even if *he* asked *me* out. After all, it hardly seems fair that the guy has to go through the agony of asking me out *and* foot the bill. Unless he insists. I'm not that benevolent.

While most people I spoke with agreed that either the person who invites should pay or you should split things 50/50, there are a few old-fashioned boys and girls out there who still insist the man should pay.

Pierre, from Montreal, holds that view: "Even if you've had the worst blind date of your life, the bill is half your credit card limit and you know you'll never call her again, you should still pull out the plastic with a big smile and insist that you want to 'take care of it.'"

Knock yourself out, buddy. Just remember – and I'm only gonna say this once – despite the root of this tradition, it's a given that, if one person foots the bill, the person being treated is under no obligation to offer a return on your investment.

Admittedly, it's kinda nice to have someone pay your way. It's also a good way to avoid having to deal with the awkwardness of dividing everything, although this can give you a good indication of how he or she is about money. If your date hauls out a calculator, it's safe to say they're a little uptight.

However, I do think that even if one person insists on paying, the other person should at least make a feeble offer to split the bill, just to be polite. Not that the person insisting should take up the offer. In fact, that would be a little tacky after insisting on paying.

And if you do decide to take someone to an expensive restaurant on a date, you should be prepared to foot the bill. It's only fair, since you picked the place.

Sometimes, paying is a good opportunity to send a message to your date. If you're less than happy with the encounter, you can absolutely insist on paying your part, even after the other person insists on covering both of you ("No, I reeeeally, reeeeally insist that I pay my share."). It's a subtle way of telling them you aren't interested and don't want to feel obligated to go out with them again.

But if it did go well, the arrival of the bill is a good opportunity to scope out the possibility of a second date. When he or she offers to pay, say, "Gee, thanks, I'll get it next time," and see how they respond.

Here's a suggestion from Sam on how to enjoy the pleasure of being treated every now and then, while still being fair. "I like to alternate paying from one date to the next," he says. "That way you both get to enjoy being spoiled, but you still share the cost."

Of course, this kind of alternating is *not* fair if she takes you to a fancy restaurant and next time you treat her to McDonald's.

One last thing. Make sure if you do plan on paying that you can. "I went out with this guy once who wanted to pay for me, but he left his wallet at home," says Sam. I guess it can happen, but talk about making a bad impression.

Finally, consider that the way you negotiate that awkward moment when the check arrives is a good indicator of how you might negotiate a relationship. Proceed with care. And make sure you have your wallet with you.

# 5

# How to Make an Impression
## Avoiding First-Date Faux Pas

There you are, scrubbed and in your best underwear, as you head off for a day of bungee jumping with the boy/girl of your dreams (or someone you can at least stand to be in the same room with). You desperately want to make a good impression; to say and do all the right things, all the while remaining cool and casual.

Relax. No one expects you to be perfect. But at least remember that, while the potential of getting laid may make some people more forgiving, there are a few things that are unforgivable on a first date (or on any other date, for that matter).

These go from the obvious – checking out other men or women, for example – to the seemingly obvious (but still incredibly not to a lot of people), like talking about past relationships on a first date. No one wants to compete with the Ghosts of Relationships Past the first time they're out with someone.

Nor does he or she want to compete with you. You know what I mean: the guy or girl who's so eager to impress, they don't shut up about themselves. Perfect first-date killer.

Ideally, we all want the first date to run smoothly and for rapport to happen perfectly naturally and spontaneously. It usually doesn't. Both of you are nervous and on your best behavior, or trying at the very least not to let one rip during a momentary lull in conversation.

If you're like most of us, the first time you're out with someone part of your brain will be busy mentally ticking off all the requirements needed to make your short list ("Let's see, funny, listens, doesn't chew with his mouth open…"). If you can, try to avoid making your checklist too obvious. You don't want your date to feel like a lab rat under observation. Or, better yet, leave the checklist at home, along with the personal agendas.

It's bad enough that the whole thing feels more like a job interview than a date – you know, if you meet the requirements, you may get a call-back. Because, on a date, as in a job interview, what you say is as important as how you say it. Your conversation skills and your body language all contribute to the impression you make. You have to try to get personal without getting too personal. You want to appear eager without overdoing it. You want to get to know the other person without putting them through the third degree. Simple, right? Here's some help.

## I've Talked Enough About Me – Now, What Do You Think of Me?

Conversation, I have always been led to believe, is meant to be an interactive activity. Sadly, some of us seem to have forgotten this basic concept.

"I was at a party and I really liked this woman," says Sarah. "Then I hear her talking to this group of people and, I swear to God, at one point she says to them all, 'Well, enough about me – let's talk about my book!' I was turned right off."

I know you know this, but I feel the need to reiterate for the conversationally challenged among us. Good conversation consists of two people talking, asking each other questions, giving more than one word answers, really listening to what the other person is saying, picking up on details and asking further questions. You don't want to turn it into an interrogation, but you need to show genuine interest. After all, isn't that why you're out with this person, because you're interested in them? And, presumably, they're interested in you. The idea is to keep it that way.

"I hate the 'So tell me about yourself' approach. That's such a cop out," says Jennifer. "I don't want to feel like I'm being interviewed. Besides, I can never remember who my favorite actor or singer is when I'm put on the spot."

So what do you talk about on a first date? It all depends on the people involved. What's fair game to one person may be taboo to another. You can usually find out what's appropriate (and what isn't) as the date progresses. You have to be sensitive to each other's boundaries. If he starts shifting uncomfortably in his seat when you ask him why he killed his family, he probably doesn't want to talk about it.

Similar interests are usually a safe place to start. Work, school, literature, food, art, music, TV, theater, current events, interesting anecdotes from your youth (and I mean *interesting*) – basically, as Ann-Marie put it, "anything that has to do with your likes, dislikes, passions and dreams usually works."

Leil Lowndes says men place more importance on having similar interests with their dates than woman do. For that reason, she says, if you want a guy to like you, and he mentions a hobby or interest, return the interest enthusiastically. Wow! I really love watching grass grow too!

Women, on the other hand, place more importance on beliefs and values. So if you want to win her over, show her you share her world view. So what if you don't exactly think obligatory castration for rapists is such a good thing.

Actually, we can usually tell if you're faking it, so don't bother if you don't really agree with her beliefs.

Having said that, it can be okay not to agree. There's nothing wrong with a little verbal sparring. Just don't try to impress the other person with the extent of your knowledge or how well you can argue a point. It's a big turn-off when someone seems more interested in being right and winning you over to their side than in respecting your opinion and at least attempting to understand where you're coming from.

"Every person brings some unique perspective to things," says Nathan. "If I'm gonna fall in love with someone, I want to fall in love with her perspective as much as I fall in love with her. We can completely disagree on something, like if we go see a movie and I thought it was a wild comedy and she thought it was a pretentious art film. But if I like how her brain works through it, how she explains her perspective to me, that can be very sexy. I want to hear more. I want to show her simple household objects and say, 'What do you think of this?' This is the kind of stuff that lets me know if I would want to spend my life with this person."

Whoa, wait a second, we're still on the first date here. I'm not thinking about spending my life with anybody just yet. Which raises the question of how intimate you should get in first-date conversation. Some people go all the way and feel nothing is off limits, but most of us are leery of getting too down-and-dirty too soon.

"I went on a date with someone who explained to me her plans for bringing up a child and where she wanted to be in five years," says Mark. "This was the first date, and I was lukewarm on the date even. A lot of women do that."

Now, now, let's be fair, Mark, some guys do it too. "We were out on our first date," says Karen, "and this guy decides he wants to be monogamous. I said, 'That's crazy! What do you mean? You can't just decide on the first date that you want a monogamous relationship with someone. You have to spend time together.' I didn't go out with him again. It was way too intense too fast."

Unfortunately, says Dr. Lila Gruzen, sometimes people are so focused on making that immediate connection, on deciding whether this person is "the one," that they get ahead of themselves. They've given the other person their entire dating history and their hopes and dreams for the future before they even know whether the other person, I dunno, likes Chinese food, for example.

"Giving too much too soon is a really easy mistake to make," Gruzen tells me over the phone from L.A., where she teaches a seminar through The Learning Annex based on her book. "People want so badly to feel intimate. They long to feel close to someone. So by the end of the first date, you've told your date everything there is to know about you, in two hours or less, without taking a breath. And you think that's being intimate, but what it's really being is premature. It just felt so good, maybe, to be with someone who was a great listener, who was a nice person, and you were kind of clicking, so you just told them way too much about yourself and your family history and your dog…"

Women make this mistake more than men, says Gruzen. That's because men are too busy trying to figure out why she doesn't turn them on. "I think men more often make the mistake of focusing too much on physical chemistry," she says. "He'll say, 'We didn't click' or 'She just wasn't for me,' and when you pin him down, more often than not that means, 'She was a great person, she was fun, she had a great a sense of humor, we got along great, but you know…she was just too short.'"

While I agree that there is such a thing as too much information too soon, it can be a good idea to get a sense of what the person wants or expects in terms of relationships in general early in the game. Especially as you get older. Who has time to mess around with someone who's not serious when you are or, conversely, if you're looking for something casual and the other person isn't? I think men get more freaked out about this stuff than women. We're more used to yammering away about our general attitude about relationships. If you ask a woman what she thinks an ideal relationship should be, even if she doesn't want to have one with you, she'll likely be willing to share her point of view.

Ask a man the same question and he'll probably run screaming from the room. Men take it more personally and seem to automatically assume that if you ask this question, you're basically asking what color he'd like the picket fence and whether the two of you should have one or two kids.

If you really want this info — and some people do like it early in the game so they can decide whether or not to waste any more time on you — Leil Lowndes suggests a less loaded way to bring it up: "Tell him your 14-year-old nephew asked you the other day what an ideal relationship should be, and you didn't know what to tell him. What does he think?"

Clever, eh? But I'd be more inclined to avoid the whole area myself, at least first time out. However, if I really wanted to get a sense of where he was in his life in terms of relationships, I'd probably just ask. If this freaks him out, I'd rather know that sooner than later.

Of course, bringing this kind of stuff up at all puts you at risk for one of those nice big awkward silences you've both been desperately trying to avoid during the date. "That's the advantage of going to a place with music and a background noise," says Mark.

Handling silences is hard. Some of us are more comfortable with them than others. "I hate silences," says Nathan. "I always scramble to fill them and it often makes it worse."

The odd silence is okay. If you're both comfortable with the occasional silence, it means you're comfortable with each other. By not rushing to fill the gaps, you don't run the risk of looking like you're trying too hard and you both get a chance to assess things, change gears, look around for the nearest exits in case things get really ugly.

Humor is always a good antidote for awkward silences or weird moments. *If* you're funny, that is. Otherwise, you'll just sound like you're trying to be funny to fill in an awkward silence.

You can also use the occasional conversation lull to say a few things in body language. If things are going well, a lingering look or a touch of the arm says plenty. In fact, body language throughout the date is an excellent way to read how things are progressing. Guys, as you get up to go pee, you

## Date from hell

I was at an art show and my friend introduced me to this woman who she thought I should go out with. We exchanged phone numbers, she gave me a call and then we met for a drink. I had just returned from my father's funeral in another city and, as it turned out, she didn't drink because she was pregnant. She asked me how I felt about dating a pregnant woman, and all I could talk about was my father's funeral and how messed up my family is. Needless to say, it didn't really work out, and we never called each other again.

could give her hand a grab and say, "I'll be right back." A well-timed grab of the knee or a gentle poke in the ribs all say, "I like how things are going here."

Verbal cues that things are going well are welcome also. If you like something the person says or does, acknowledge it. I'm amazed at how stingy we can be with compliments. And I don't mean your run-of-the-mill, "you've got beautiful eyes" stuff. Too much smarm potential with these kinds of comments. I'm talking about appreciating someone's uniqueness. If they say something you think is smart, tell them; if they say something funny, laugh and tell them you think they're funny. We all like our egos stroked, especially if it's genuine. And if you're having a good time, why not thank the person for inviting you, before the date's over, so they know things are going well?

The best way to make an impression on a date is to try not to make an impression. It is not a performance. There's a difference between trying to do the right things to make a date go well and trying to make yourself look good. What is impressive is someone who puts us at ease, who seems comfortable and can make other people feel comfortable and who's considerate and confident. Dating can be tense, and someone who can relieve the tension will score big points.

If you master all this and things do go well on the first date, be careful not to become too cocky. Your foot's in the door, but you're far from home-free. At this delicate stage in the game, things could still go either way. You have to play it cool. Don't blow it by coming on too strong. Wanting to get together again too soon or calling sixteen times a day to tell the person what a great time you had on your first date might be a bit of a turn-off. Relax. You've got time. Wait at least until he or she can't live without you before you show them your true clingy, needy self.

# First Date Conversation No-No's

What not to talk about on a first date:

- "Diseases or illnesses, obsessive behavior, friends in jail."

- "Exes."

- "Medical problems that mean he can't have children. (It happened. Honest.)"

- "Bodily functions."

- "Details about failed personal relationships."

- "How much you hate your family."

- "How you were dumped by all your former girlfriends."

- "Politics, religion or sexuality." (Jeez, tough customer.)

- "Family problems."

- "Your favorite sexual positions."

- "Past boyfriends, past dates, dead cats, negative ideas."

- "Cars. Some guys can talk about their goddamn vehicle for hours." (I hear ya. Unless you're a car freak too, car talk is boring!)

- "How much money you make or spend."

- "Financial difficulties."

- "How I should run my life, according to you!"

- "Premature ejaculation." (Seriously, folks, get with it.)

## Communication Rules

Before you open your mouth, keep these basic first-date conversation rules in mind.

1. Don't say stuff you don't mean. Telling someone you like them more than you actually do just so you can sleep with them is cruel and disrespectful. Making someone believe they have a chance with you when you're really just enjoying their attention and have no intention of going out with them again is also nasty.

2. Don't assume anything. Don't assume, for example, that you have a chance with someone just because they seem to be enjoying your attention. Don't assume that just because someone is talking to you that you're having a meaningful conversation. Some people are just polite.

3. Listen. No, reeeally listen. You might even want to repeat things back to the person in your own words once in a while to let them know you've really heard them.

4. Don't impose your ideas on someone. Telling someone that you think their friends are imbeciles probably won't endear you to them. Even if their friends really are imbeciles.

5. Don't project your idea of someone onto them. You might think that you're being helpful by telling someone all the ways you think they are wasting their life and how they deserve better. You aren't.

6. Don't say, "I'll call you," if you have no intention of doing so.

## Lasting Impressions

Some dates leave more of an impression than others. And sometimes the impression isn't necessarily so positive. Here are some memorable, and highly unimpressive, dating moments, courtesy of some of the people I spoke to.

**On making someone feel uncomfortable:** "I went out with this guy and I was wearing a blue dress. He wouldn't walk with me, instead he walked several steps behind. He finally said, 'That dress falls really nicely.' Then he asked if he could touch it. It was like a *Seinfeld* episode."

**On not listening:** "He was a nice guy, but he didn't really listen to me most of the time during our date. At some points, I would say something and he would just keep talking as if I hadn't uttered a word. He is a drummer, so I thought maybe he was a bit deaf, but I don't know. Despite this, he seemed to think things were going quite well. I was freaking out by the end of the evening. I didn't even want to kiss him, much less have intimate physical relations of other kinds. I didn't know that to do. We were at a pub and I drank something like five whiskeys and felt totally sober. Not even my old friend the bottle could loosen me up."

**On fabricating interesting things about yourself:** "I didn't really want to go out with this guy but I thought, what the hell, I'll go out for dinner. For some reason I decided I was going to tell him I was a kick-boxer, which was so stupid because I know nothing about it. And then he drops casually in conversation – luckily before I brought it up – 'Did you know I'm a kick-boxer?' Turns out he was a kick-boxing champion."

**On boring your date to tears:** "He re-enacted the last seven days of Pompeii. I'm serious!"

**On bringing other relationships to the date:** "I went out with this woman, but she didn't tell me that she hadn't quite ended her previous relationship. We were back at her place after our first date, and the phone rings and she goes into the other room to answer it. After she hung up, she yells, 'You have to leave the apartment now! My boyfriend's coming over.' Really uncool."

**On what not to talk about on a date:** "This guy I went out with was really into the subject of mind control. On our first date, that's all he talked about all night. He was also really into conspiracy theories and was going on about how the government has us all brainwashed. It was interesting for about a minute. A whole evening of it was excruciating."

**On bringing friends on dates:** "I asked her if she wanted to go see a band with me, and she asked if I minded if some friends of hers came along because she hadn't seen them in a while. I was thinking, 'Oooh-kayyy…' Well, I showed up, and they were quite late, and I ended up spending only about five or ten minutes talking to this woman the whole night. She was totally absorbed in talking to her friends, and it really pissed me off. I phoned her the next day and told her that I was pretty hurt about it, and she just made an excuse, saying she was drunk or something. Things didn't work out with her, to say the least."

**On casting the net too wide just to see what you'll pull in:** "This guy I knew really wanted to be in a relationship. We decided to go out once, but it wasn't really clear if it was a date. When I showed up at the bar to meet him, he was flirting with the waitress. I'm thinking to myself, 'Lesson No. 1, buddy: Do not flirt with the waitress when the person you kind of, might be dating walks in.' I quickly decided I didn't want it to be a date and I did everything I could do to act like it was not a date. At one point, I just came out and told him I didn't think of this as a date. His response was, 'Oh, well, what about that friend of yours I met last week? Can I get her phone number from you?' Desperate, or what?"

**On dating accessories:** "When I went on my first date with this guy, he brought a bag of pistachios with him. We went to the movies, and he started eating these nuts and dropping the shells on the floor. I wasn't sure what bugged me more, the noise he was making eating the nuts or the mess he was making on the floor."

On making your date feel insignificant: "It was our first date and we decided to meet at this bar. I walk in and she's reading a magazine, and she keeps on flipping through the magazine even after I arrive. I was like, 'Excuse me? I have arrived.' But she kept flipping through the magazine. I ordered a drink, but I thought, 'If she flips one more page of that magazine, I'm outta here.' She eventually stopped, but I was not impressed."

# 6

# Wanna Come Up for a Drink?

## Going All the Way

And now for the whole point of dating: Sex. Yeah, yeah, I know, it's not just about sex, it's about compatibility, whether the person makes you laugh, whether you think you could stand waking up beside them naked. Like I said...whether you're gonna get any or not lingers over the whole event like the garlic you ate too much of at dinner because you had nothing to say.

You may not do the deed that night, but whether you can imagine sex with this person at some point and whether they can imagine it with you is pretty much what we're aiming for here. You may both be into yogic flying, love mushroom soup and tuna on toast and think *Entertainment Tonight* is high art, but if there's no sexual chemistry, well, you might as well resign yourself to the fact that the most you're gonna get out of this is maybe a new pal.

Sometimes sexual chemistry is there right off the bat. Often indicated by the tingling you get in your groin when he or she is within drooling distance. Sometimes it takes a little time to recognize. I didn't realize I had unawakened lustful thoughts about one guy I went out with until after he puked at a party one night. I dunno, he just looked so darn cute and vulnerable all passed out on the floor afterwards.

Of course, what you do with sexual chemistry is another thing. I didn't have sex with Vomit Boy for at least another month. There's a lot to be said for holding off on sex when you start dating someone new. There's also something to be said for jumping in the sack right away.

Even if you do wait, that doesn't mean you can't have lots of other frisky fun in the meantime. Sometimes there's no need to wait because sex is all you're after and a one-night stand will do just fine, thank you very much. At the other extreme, there are still some of you out there holding off on sex completely, at least until you're married.

## Like a Virgin: Yes, There Are Still a Few Left

Should you or shouldn't you? As long as young people have dated, the question of if and when to have sex has been an issue. And adults have tried to influence the answer. Especially if you're a girl.

In *From Front Porch to Back Seat*, author Beth L. Bailey quotes a husband-hunting manual from 1945: "Remember that the average man will go as far as you let him go. A man is only as bad as the woman he is with."

In other words, good girls don't. Or didn't.

Of course, not all of us fell for the good-girl routine. In fact, by the time I started dating in the seventies, we were so casual about sex that you usually did "it" even before you did coffee. In the eighties, the rise of AIDS put the brakes on that. (Thank God. The shag-rug burns were doing me in.) And the rise of the Christian right brought back those old-fashioned values. The rise of a new chastity movement has convinced some young people to wait until marriage. Even those who couldn't wait can now redeem themselves with born-again virgin status if they vow not to do it again until marriage. And, with an increasingly multicultural society, more and more young people are having to deal with the clash between what the kids at school are doing and what their more traditional folks at home expect. Like the group of 17- and 18-year-old women I spoke to who come from Asian and Arabic backgrounds. Their families have taught them that sex before marriage is a sin. As a result, they believe sex is not to be taken lightly.

"It's precious," says 17-year-old Jen, a first-generation Chinese-Canadian whose parents don't even want her to date, much less have sex. "The first time has to be beautiful, not just because I'm horny and we decide to just go for it."

"I'll probably have sex before marriage, but after I'd feel bad about it," adds 18-year-old Nathalie, from a strict Muslim background. "You know, the guilt. I would feel low. I want it to be with someone who loves me, who really, really loves me."

Don't we all, honey? I mean, I see some value in holding out, mostly for your physical and emotional health. But jeez, I'm 34 and not married. A girl only has so much willpower!

Predictably, the young guys I spoke to weren't quite so protective of their virginity. "Maybe it's their outdoor plumbing," Nathalie suggested. Ah, the old "because it is there" attitude. To their credit, though, the guys did say they prefer to at least like the person before they have sex.

"Waiting is a big thing for a lot of girls," says Sandy. "Most guys I know want it to mean something. Not necessarily marriage, but if you're gonna have sex, you want more than just the physical gratification."

Of course, despite the strong messages to wait until you're ready, most young people these days definitely don't wait until marriage. Times haven't changed that much.

The question is, how long do you wait?

## Sex on the First Date?

I was on a panel talking about dating and one of the male guests said that a woman could make a guy like her if she didn't sleep with him right away. "Man," I thought to myself, "haven't we gotten over this yet?" "Make yourself scarce and watch your value go up" was the advice given to young ladies in the *Ladies' Home Journal* in 1942, according to Beth L. Bailey's book. That was over 50 years ago. Surely, guys don't still have this notion that you sleep with one kind of girl and "date" another?

"It would just make me wonder if she slept with every guy that easily" was my co-panelist's response. Of course, if a guy slept with every woman that easily, he'd be Mr. Stud. She's just easy. Sad to say, that old double standard is also still alive and well.

All right, I've calmed down. And yes, you're probably right, as much as there are definite lingerings of that "good girl, bad girl" mentality, I think most men and women do tend to have two categories for the people they go out with: people you sleep with and people you have a relationship with. But for women, I think deciding not to sleep with someone is less of a value judgment than a question of not wanting to make yourself physically vulnerable to someone before you're ready.

"I don't want to sleep with people in the relationship category if it's not going to go anywhere, because it's potentially too devastating," says Sarah.

Still, I think it's safe to say that, whether you're a stud or a slut, the novelty of casual sex does seems to wear off as you get older. "As I get into my 30s, I'm less likely to sleep with people right away, especially if I don't want a relationship," says Jennifer. "I end up feeling really shitty afterwards. And it's not a moral thing or because I want more from that person. It just drives home what I'm missing."

I can relate. As I get older, I also find myself holding off (at least until the second date) with the guys I like. It's partly for health reasons, but mostly its because sleeping with someone can really change the playing field and mess with your judgment. Once he's seen your saddlebags, it's tough to go back to small talk.

Even guys get wise to this as they age. And they don't even get saddlebags.

"Even though I may want to have sex on the first date, I've always felt that it skews my perception of that person," says Tom. "Too many times, first dates have ended up in bed, followed by a relationship based on sex, followed by the discovery that the relationship was hollow. I prefer to date a couple of times before consummating a budding relationship, if only to know that I will feel comfortable doing other things than making love all the time." Yeah, you know how rough that can be.

"I think the biggest problem is that if you do have sex and it's any good, you start fantasizing, thinking too much about the future," says Lise. "I'm better at seeing things more realistically now. I might think, 'Okay, that was great. Good start,' but I try not to envision my entire future based on one sexual encounter."

That's not to say that there aren't merits to sleeping with someone right away. As Sarah says, sometimes there are people you just want to sleep with and you know there is no relationship potential. The attraction is purely physical and if you can keep your head about it, you can have some fun. I for one am sometimes glad to do away with all the preciousness of it and just enjoy a good romp once in a while. As a woman, it can be very liberating.

"You're taught it's the most sacred thing you can give," Tara laughs. "Oh well! I just gave it to some guy that I met an hour ago!"

## To Wait or Not to Wait?

That is the question. Here are some of the answers I received.

**Wait:**

- "I think it can wait if he is a keeper."

- "Sex on a first date: not a good idea. Play hard to get. Think about it this way: lions don't chase dead meat."

- "If you appear too easy you look desperate. People who haven't had sex for a long time, or a boyfriend for a long time, they get this look of desperation on their face. You know the look. It scares me off."

- "I won't have sex if I want to see him again. Because if I do have sex with him, and we don't see each other again, it'll really hurt."

- "I've always regretted the relationships that have started with sleeping together on the first date. We go out and I think, 'Oh well, I haven't been laid in so long…You're pretty cute and sort of cool…We'll see what happens,' and I sleep with him. Next thing I know, I'm in a relationship. It's like a one-night stand that got out of control."

- "Because of the whole AIDS scare, I tell myself I should get to know people, so I should at least wait until the third date, or preferably the fifth date, before I sleep with someone. Unfortunately, I've broken my own rule lots of times."

**Don't Wait:**

- "If there is no real potential for a relationship, but you are attracted to each other, why not?"

- "I don't mess around with trying to be demure. If I'm attracted to someone, it doesn't matter if it's the first date or the 10th – sex is good."

- "I think you have to like having sex with someone right away. Personally, I wouldn't date somebody who I didn't enjoy having sex with. Because if you don't like having sex with them, what do you do for the first three months of your relationship?"

- "It's a great way to get to know each other. I think people are much more relaxed lying in bed naked, having sex and then talking about themselves than they are sitting in a bar or buying groceries."

- "You might not be as sexually attracted to the person the next day. You might as well strike while the iron is hot, as it were."

- "You might get hit by a bus tomorrow."

## All the Fun's in the Fumbling:
## Just Fooling Around

Just because you don't have sex on the first date, there is definitely no need to go home empty-handed. Whether it's a tender, heartfelt kiss at the end of the night or a full make-out session, there's plenty of truth to that old phrase, "All the fun's in the fumbling." Not to be confused, however, with "bundling" – something they did back in colonial times.

Bundling was a practice in the U.S. in colonial times, in which a woman would invite her date to sleep in the same bed with her, only they'd stay fully clothed. Often a board would be placed between their bodies as a barrier. Why they called this bundling, I have no idea. But what a way to build sexual tension.

While there are easier ways to go about it, there is definitely something to be said for showing a little restraint when you're out on a date. (Just don't show so much restraint that you both go home alone, scratching your heads, trying to figure out what it all meant.) Holding back can really heat things up. It's like extended foreplay, and it can be oh so delicious. For example:

"For six weeks we'd go cycling every weekend," says Elizabeth. "Slowly, these little rituals developed. One week, I brought soup, the next week she brought wine and crackers, then I brought Smarties. She showed so much restraint, going home in the early evening with nothing more than a peck on the cheek. It was excruciating.

"Then this one weekend, I had the worst period of my life. I was bloated and bleeding, and I almost canceled our date. But I couldn't resist. We're out and it got to be 10 at night, then 11, then 11:30. We're having coffee at this greasy spoon, and at one point I put my arm across the table and she lay her head on it. I thought I was going to die. This was after six weeks.

"And then she says, 'Can I come home with you?' and I say, 'Um, tonight?' She says, 'Oh, you don't feel the same way I do.' And I say, 'Of course I do, but I'm having the worst period of my life. I cannot sleep with you for the first time while I'm holding 10 pounds of water.' And she answers, 'Oh shit, now I have to wait another week.' And that's when I realized that she had been feeling the same way."

Gets me all weepy, that story does.

The problem, often, is that it can be difficult to know if, when and how to make a move. You're being cautious because: What if the feeling isn't mutual? What if the other person doesn't respond? What if you've got it all wrong and this really isn't a "date" and if you try to put the moves on her, she'll double over laughing?

So how do you know when to make a move? "I'm pretty good at reading body language," says Jeff, "but to this day, making a move is a 100 percent gamble in my opinion. Luckily, I've won the gamble more times then I've lost, because I usually wait for her to move first."

Well, with those kind of odds…

"I never make the first move because I never know when is a good time," says Hillary, a shy 26-year-old reference librarian. See what I mean? Even if the sparks are about to ignite the curtains because the sexual chemistry between you is so strong, it's still hard to know how far the other person is willing to go.

This is usually the point where I ask him up to my place for a drink. Beverages play a big role in taking the sexual energy up a notch. "Especially if she invites you up for coffee and you told her previously that you don't drink cof-

## Date from Hell

When I was in school this friend of mine had a roommate who I didn't think much of until I ran into him years later and he looked really good. He had a goatee and longish hair. Anyway, he ended up calling me and inviting me to a classmate's house for dinner. It was nice, so when he called again and invited me over to his place to watch a movie, I didn't think twice about it. Problem was, when he picked me up I saw that he had cut his hair. That wasn't so bad, but he had also shaved off his goatee. That pretty much killed it. Sexual attraction: gone. After the movie he was obviously ready to do the horizontal mambo. He stuck his tongue in my mouth (a stinky, smoky tongue, I might add) and then he started to devour my neck. I told him that I bruise easily, so please, no hickeys. Sure enough, when I got home I saw that I had a hickey on my neck! That was it: it was over. My friend told me later that the hickey demon couldn't figure out why I had stopped calling. Sheeeeesh!

fee," laughs Martin. Inviting someone up for tea, a nightcap, a stiff Scotch – all are code for, "I want to screw you silly," or at least, "I'm open to the suggestion."

Because remember, we're supposed to be showing restraint here. When I do invite someone over, I make sure I'm clear in my mind about how far I want things to go…and then I end up sleeping with him anyway. No, really, it can be wonderfully exciting to make out like a couple of teenagers and then pull your disheveled selves together, say good night and go to bed (alone) where you can dream up the rest in your head.

But you don't even have to get that far your first time out. Sometimes, all you need is a well-timed kiss at the end of the evening. I love that moment when you're just dying to kiss the other person. You're looking at him, half listening to him ramble on about God knows what and at some point you simply lean in and kiss him. There's something very exhilarating about just going for it. Taking the other person by surprise and diving in.

Just make sure you've tested the waters first. If she's sitting six feet away from you and cringes every time your arms touch, you'd best stay on shore. If, on the other hand, he holds your gaze every once in a while, or you find him staring at you out of the corner of your eye with a shit-eating grin on his face, jump in.

But always keep in mind that a first kiss is like a handshake. It says a lot about what else you have to offer. Warm and tender, firm yet gentle. And no slobbering or sudden deep-tongue dives. Gagging can be a real turn-off.

## One-Night Wonders: When Sex Is All You're After

Of course, sometimes you want to throw restraint out the window, forget about whether you'll ever see each other again and just have sex – no strings attached. Plenty of you agreed that there is a time and a place for one-night stands. As long as it is clear and understood for what it is. One night, no strings, breakfast not included. C'mon, admit it, you've done it. Okay, so some of us actually haven't. Before you get all uppity on the rest of us, consider some of the benefits.

It's great for a little human contact when you're running short. "One-night stands are part of life and normal for people who are not in a relationship but would like some affection now and then," says Ann-Marie.

Or a little sex. "I'm in a phase right now where I don't want a relationship," says John. "Just good sex."

Not to say that a one-night stand guarantees good sex. "There's too much bullshit involved for one night of sex, bad sex usually," says Karen. "And it's not necessarily any easier to find someone for a one-night stand than for a relationship."

That's probably because even if it's only for one night, a girl's got standards. "Even a one-night stand has to be with someone I like as a friend, who I respect, who I think is a good person," says Jennifer.

Is it just me or isn't that exactly what you're *not* looking for in a one-night stand? But yes, even I admit that one-night stands do somehow lose their luster as you get older and your standards get tougher.

"I have no problem with the idea of one-night stands," says Sarah. "But I find it's harder to appreciate them as you get older. I think it's because you become pickier about who you want to spend your time with, even if it is for one night."

And even if it's only a one-off screw, it can still screw with your head. "I think I'm too emotional for one-night stands," says Tom. "The last few have left me pretty messed up."

Others are quite simply against the whole concept and won't do it...at least not again. "Call me old-fashioned, but the last time I did it, I felt cheapened," says Karen. "That was the last time for me."

"They're great at the time," says Caroline. "A great way to expunge that carnal need for a while, at least. Still, I've found relationship sex to be much better. It's more intimate and there's no guilt. But I can't seem to stop myself from seeking out casual sex once in a while. Just a stupid primate, I suppose."

There's no denying that sometimes, one-night stands get ugly. "I've been kicked out of guys' beds in the middle of the night after sex because they don't want you there in the morning," says Tara. "That was mostly when I was in my early 20s, back in university. That's really gross."

Those are the ones that often involve alcohol. "I try to avoid having sex with a guy when I'm drunk," Tara continues. "Drunken one-night stands are bad, bad, bad."

Especially when you have to work in the morning…together.

"I woke up with a co-worker after a night of drinking and neither one of us remembered anything," Sam admits. "At least there was a condom on the floor."

## Happy Hour: Mixing Sex and Alcohol

Getting drunk and making a fool of yourself is definitely not a good way to make an impression on your first date. But, let's face it, "alcohol is a popular social lubricant," as a sex educator I spoke to once said. K-Y for the mind, if you like. A little social lube and insecurities, judgment, motor skills and that nasty grip on reality just slip away. It's beautiful, really.

And the big advantage to hitting the sauce on a date is that it increases your odds of getting some. Because, as you may well know, standards go out the window when you're drunk. Once you've got yer "beer goggles" on people you'd never think of sleeping with when you're sober suddenly seem way hot.

If you do manage to get lucky after tossing back a few, drunk sex can actually be a lot of fun, since drinking lowers inhibitions and encourages you to flaunt all your tacky porn-star aspirations (plus double vision lets you fulfill your fantasy of having a threesome when there's only two of you). If you're really lucky, in the morning maybe one of you will even remember how great it was.

However, it's all fun and games until some guy tries to use his drunkenness as a defense when he gets charged with sexual assault. Nice try, buddy, but drunkenness does not give you license to do anything against anyone's will.

Plenty of us have done stuff we've regretted when we were drunk. And lots of us have embarrassing drunken-sex stories. I've even had sex when I didn't necessarily want to, but we were both drunk and it just seemed easier at the time. Not very savory, I admit, but shit happens. Still, I always knew I could say no. That's the difference, and it's a biggie. Last I heard, when you have sex with someone against their will (no matter how smashed you are), they call it rape.

This still seems to be the toughest lesson on some university campuses, where the course of choice is "Drinking and Sex 101." Learning to mix drinks and sex drives is volatile. You want so much to believe that "no" somehow reeeally means "yes" or at least "maybe, with some convincing." You can't figure out how she could be all over you all night but then not wanna have sex with you. Well, guess what? She can. "No" really does means "no," and if someone is too drunk to utter that little word, why not be really mature and make that executive decision for them?

Remembering to slip on that little piece of rubber is another thing that often slips our minds when we're drunk. "I'll save my life next time" can seem like such rational thinking in the heat of the moment. The best thing to do is to somehow program this into your auto-pilot. A friend told me he realized he had mastered this when he was with someone and was so drunk he could barely speak. "I was saying, 'cuh-duh, cuh-duh,' and the guy I was with was like, 'Huh?' Finally he realized I was trying to say 'con-dom.' He pulled one out, slipped it on and off we went."

Now there's a quality drunken sexual experience. Cheers!

## Playin' It Safe: Don't Forget to Wear Your Rubbers

Which brings us to the issue of safe sex. You'd think, after almost two decades of safe-sex messages, practising it would be a given by now. But obviously, from what I hear out there, it isn't. Mind you, people still smoke – even though that'll kill ya too.

Here's the deal. Condoms are a must, whether it's your first date or your 50th. Okay, maybe by your 50th, if you're both committed and monogamous (not just in theory but in practice, and are willing to admit it if you slip), you've both been tested (for AIDS and other STDs) and – if you're hetero – are using another form of birth control, maybe then, and only then, can you lose the raincoat. Is that clear?

I'm sad to report that plenty of us are still being irresponsible when it comes to safe sex. We're still afraid to bring it up, and guys still use that old "I can't come with a condom" routine. Sometimes we're just plain lazy about it. And we still have this notion that safe sex isn't sexy. As my dear friend Audrey always says, "What's not sexy about feeling safe?"

Whether gay or straight, I think we lull ourselves into a false sense of security. You know what I mean. You have sex with someone a few times, and when neither of you develops AIDS within two weeks, you somehow convince yourself it might be okay to ride bareback once in a while. It's scary. How in denial are we about AIDS if people can slip into this kind of behavior? We foolishly act as though it's curable. (Not to mention the rise in other STDs, such as herpes, and unwanted pregnancies.)

And guys, if you think condoms are a drag, try using a dental dam sometime! "It's not sexy at all as a lesbian to have safe sex," complains Helen, a 30-year-old lesbian and lab technician. "Dental dams taste terrible, and you can't feel anything through them. I had this lover who snapped a rubber glove on her hand thinking she was being all sexy, and I was like, 'yech.'"

Okay, so perhaps the safe-sex options are a tad underdeveloped for the lesbian set. Luckily, lesbians are way lower on the risk scale. Not that that's an excuse. You just never know where she's been.

Bottom line: since sexual history doesn't exactly make great first-date conversation, it's best to look out for yourself. Don't rely on your partner to come clean. Insist on a condom. Ultimately, everyone is responsible for their own safety.

As far as I'm concerned, someone who's concerned about their own health is pretty sexy. And consider this, guys: if potential sterility (from certain STDs), parenthood or death aren't incentive enough, think of the impression you'll make. Chicks love it when you bring up the safe-sex thing. Plus, if you bring your own rubber, you get to use your favorite brand.

# 7

# Is This a Date?
## When You're Just Not Sure...

At least if you hop in the sack with someone at the end of a first date, it's pretty clear that there's some chemistry. But what if you go out with someone and it's not even clear if it's a date? There you are, "out for a drink after work" or some equally ambiguous activity, actin' all casual so you won't feel like an idiot if it turns out you're *not* on a date. Then the other person, who's been thinking it's a date all along, figures since you're being so casual, you must not consider it a date and aren't interested. Crazy stuff. We end up casualties of our own casual attitude about dating.

Some might say it's a small price to pay to protect ourselves from the embarrassment and pain of assuming too much. But I'm not so sure.

"I wish things were a little bit more up front – you know, 'Okay, this is a DATE!'" complains 31-year-old Kevin, a graphic designer who admits to being pretty clueless about dating. "Back in the fifties, if you liked somebody, you asked them out on a date and they accepted or not. The lines were distinctly drawn, and there wasn't that weird kind of uncertainty that there is now."

We hear ya, Kevin. These days, if you "go for coffee," half the time you have no idea what that means. These casual boundaries can be nice for a little leeway, but there are times when this blurriness can create problems.

Like when you work at a record store and a customer asks you to go to a concert with him and you say "Yes" – even though you have a boyfriend. "This guy used to come into the store all the time and we'd chat and I just figured that, since I was planning on going to the concert anyway, it made sense," says Lise. "I even suggested we meet for a drink beforehand. It didn't occur to me until afterwards that he was maybe asking me on a date. I went anyway and there we were, just hanging out, when my boyfriend shows up. The guy never really talked to me after that."

It can be a bit of a problem when you think the two of you are just hanging out as "friends" and the other person, well, the other person doesn't.

"I end up in a lot of stupid situations where I like someone as a friend and they think I'm dating them, or vice-versa," says Nathan. "I have some very close female friends, but I also like to date women. Sometimes it's not clear to some of these female friends – or even to me – what we're doing. It can be a real adventure sorting it out."

It can be even more confusing if you're a woman who likes to date women. "If you're a woman out with a guy, I think it's more clear it's a date because the roles between men and women are so rigidly defined," Sarah speculates. "Whereas with women, I don't think I always know if it's a date. If the woman is gay, it doesn't mean that she's necessarily interested in me. The codes are more subtle and it's often hard to tell. You almost want to just come right out and say, 'You know, I'm kind of interested in the possibility of this going somewhere. I don't know if you are, and if you're not, that's fine, I'm happy to be friends.'"

The problem is, most of us would be terrified to put ourselves on the line like that. "Ya know, I kinda like you. And if you can't stand me that's okay, but I thought I'd just throw that out there." Ack!

It can be pretty frightening too, if one of you suddenly tries to define whatever it is you're doing. "We'd been out before, but they weren't dates, just getting together after work," Tom remembers. "We were drinking wine, having a good time, and I wasn't thinking about her too hard because I wasn't in the mood to attach myself to anyone. Then we're walking home, she makes a joke and I put my arm around her, just as a friendly gesture. Next thing, I look over and she's practically on the other side of the street. I think it scared her."

## Going in Blind

Speaking of scary, can we talk about blind dates for a minute? Can't say I've ever had the pleasure myself, but apparently people still subject themselves to this form of cruelty.

"My dad went to Greece and met this guy he really liked," says Alex, whose background is Greek. "He figured this guy and I were a great match. He had a good job, was my age and he was Greek! I couldn't help think that if my dad liked him so much maybe *he* should date him. But I wasn't getting much action at the time so I figured, what the hell. I was hoping that we would at least write or talk to each other before there was any kind of major step made, but the guy wanted to meet me right away. So he just picked up and came over here – in the middle of February!

"It was nerve-wracking, because I had no idea what his expectations were. I tried to make it as clear as possible that we were just going to suss each other out. I didn't make any promises to anybody. At the same time, part of me thought, 'Hey, you never know.' I went with my parents to pick him up at the airport. Of course, first glance and I thought, 'Totally not for me!'"

Alex dragged her brother out with them on their first "date." Even so, her visitor didn't exactly get the hint. "He mentioned a few times that we should go out again, but I just said, 'Well, I'm pretty happy in my life here and you would have a hard time adjusting and I don't think it will work. Nice to have met you. Have a safe trip back.'"

Ah, that old "We live in different countries" line.

They don't call 'em blind dates for nothing. It almost seems mandatory that they have to involve the two most mismatched people in the world.

"I've gone on two blind dates," Ann-Marie admits. "I'm never going on any more, and I shouldn't even have gone on the second one. You know what a blind date is? It's getting together with a complete stranger and deciding if you want to sleep together. That's what you're doing. You're checking each other out, with no one else there to distract you."

Karen had a really weird experience. "An old friend – I'll call him Keith – set me up with his best friend," she says. "But when Keith's friend called me up, he sounded just like Keith. He says, 'Keith said I should call you.' I thought it was Keith just pulling my leg and I went along with it, thinking it was Keith's way of asking me out. Finally the big evening rolls around and the doorbell rings. I open the door, and it is a complete stranger. I felt like such an idiot because I'd been looking forward to a reunion dinner with Keith."

To make things worse, Keith's friend was wearing white socks and running shoes with a turtleneck and blazer…and, yes, a kerchief in his blazer pocket. Yow! "I think he was trying to dress up for dinner."

"We went for dinner," Karen continues. "He took me to this place where they served turtles. Real turtles. Not the chocolates. It was quite delicious. I was wearing a little black dress and big boots – my usual garb – and he thought I was some crazy downtown bohemian girl. I asked if we could sit in the smoking section, and he says 'Oooh, bad girl smokes!' And I'm thinking, 'Eeew, don't say that. It makes me want to smoke more and kill you.'

"This restaurant was a bring-your-own-wine place. Liquor was definitely required in this situation. After dinner, we ran out of stuff to drink. He wanted to go out for another drink but I said no, and he took me home. Of course, 20 minutes later I went out for another drink with some friends."

The poor guy obviously thought it went better than she did, because he called her every day for about a week afterwards.

"He wouldn't leave a message when he called and I would do the '∗69' thing to trace his call. Every single time, the number was some hospital. Finally, I put it together. He worked at the hospital."

The "∗69" trick really does take all the fun out of being obsessive, doesn't it? Just a note: obsessive behavior doesn't qualify as dating. Generally, dating requires the consent of both parties. I know you may think that it will only take that 456th call to convince him or her that you are meant to be together, but chances are it will only convince the person that you're completely nuts. Not such a big turn-on.

I'm sure it's possible to have a successful blind date. It's also possible to lick pavement. But why put yourself through it when there are so many other more pleasant ways to punish yourself? Like chewing on glass.

Consider the agony Jennifer could've saved herself from. "After several calls back and forth, with me basically postponing the date as long as possible, we finally went to a movie," she says. "We were to meet at the movie theater. I had no idea what he looked like. So I go and there's a guy standing there, and I'm thinking, 'It definitely can't be that guy. I wouldn't be attracted to that guy. But he's the only guy there. Yup, it's the guy.'"

Personally, I probably would have hightailed it out of there but, hey, I'm a wuss, and polite girl that she is, Jennifer decided to go through with it.

"I knew as soon as I met him that he wasn't my type, and I could tell he didn't think I was his type either. But we go into the movie and he knows that I work in film, so during the trailers he's asking all these questions. I hate talking during movies, even trailers. Finally he shuts up and we're both sitting there and it's really awkward. At one point my elbow touched his and I was like, 'Uuuuugh, get it away.'

"After the movie, he drove me home and he says 'So, do you like music?' I'm thinking. 'Yeah. So do you like breathing?!' I don't understand the question. Of course I like music.' Then we got to my place and he says, 'That was nice, give me a call,' and I was like 'okay' or 'you give me a call.' But we both knew it was a disaster, we were just too polite to say it. Needless to say, I never heard from him again. That was when I realized I just have to stop saying yes to blind dates.

"At the time you think, 'It'll be fine, a bit of an adventure.' And I guess it was a bit of adventure, I did milk that story for quite a while after it happened. But it was incredibly uncomfortable. We didn't like each other. There was no spark, we had nothing to say. It was a real drag. We shouldn't have let ourselves be put in that position."

You said it, Jennifer, not me.

## Just as Friends?

Dating friends is another tricky one. My own experience of trying to get more friendly with a friend was ugly. It was back in high school. I invited a buddy of an ex-boyfriend to the grad, "just as friends." I'd been lusting after him for a while but I knew his loyalty to my ex would preclude me from asking him on an actual date. I figured I could play along with the "just friends" bit, then ply him with alcohol and take advantage of him. It worked (remember, kids: loyalty and alcohol don't mix). But even as we were going at it in the plush surroundings of his shag-carpeted van, I knew it was trouble. Sure enough, he regretted his actions by the sober light of day and, worse still, our friendship was never the same again.

Sleeping with friends is risky, even if you're both into it. Because, no matter how many times you say you don't want to screw up your friendship by sleeping together, you usually do. And, lucky you, since it usually doesn't pan out as a sexual relationship, you get two for the price of one: a screwed-up relationship and a screwed-up friendship. Sure, over time, the weirdness subsides and you can usually re-establish some semblance of friendship, but it's never the same after you've seen 'em naked.

Even if you don't end up sleeping together, once you mess with the platonic status of a friendship, it's tough to go back. It's easier if you both realize you're better off as friends, but if the push to become "more than friends" is one-sided, the ensuing scenario is not gonna be pretty.

"I was friends with this woman and at one point we thought there might be something more to it," John says. "We decided to try and date. She was into it, but I quickly realized I liked her better as a friend. I told her and we tried to stay friends, but there was always this underlying feeling I got from her that she was hoping things would change, that I'd eventually see how great she was and come round. I didn't and we're no longer friends."

It can be confusing. If you have friends of the opposite sex and you're straight, it's hard not to wonder at some point why it wouldn't work as a relationship. It's even worse if you're gay, because your friends are more often the same gender as the people you date.

At some point in the friendship, you're bound to check out each other with that look in your eyes that says, "Is something happening here?" "Could something happen here?" "I like everything about this person, why don't I want to sleep with them? Hmm…Let me sleep with them and find out. Oh, now I see why. Shit."

Mind you, when you can make the successful leap from friends to lovers, it's great. Mainly because you've already mastered what so many of us neglect to do with the people we date: get to know each other and become friends before worrying about whether we want two kids together or three.

## Date from Hell

One Saturday this guy I worked with called and invited me to a concert. I really wanted to see the show, so I jokingly asked him, "What happened? Did your date fall through?" Turns out it actually had, so I told him I'd go. In my mind this was not a date, it was me bailing this guy out. He had an extra ticket, and I thought I'd made it very clear that I wasn't interested in him other than as a friend.

We went to the concert and it was really great, so afterwards we went for a drink. Then he started saying stuff like, "Oh, you don't ski. But it would be so wonderful if we could ski together. Afterwards there'd be an open fire…" He started describing this whole romantic seduction scenario, and I was thinking, "Uuugggh!" Then he said, "Are you attracted to me?" Uuugggh again! I told him I thought of him entirely as a friend, and he said, "Well, if this isn't going anywhere, I don't want to waste my time." I couldn't believe it! I turned into my mother and completely chewed him out. He totally ruined the whole concert experience for me!

## Fling Fever

Flings probably merit a brief mention here. Flings fall in a different category than dating. They're all about indulgence – a brief, pleasurable dalliance. There's often plenty of chemistry, but little future and you both know and are okay with that.

More often than not, flings are sexually based. Unlike a one-night stand, however, you want to have sex with the person more than once. But you don't want to have a relationship with them for whatever reason – say, because they're moving to Mexico.

"A fling is based on purely sexual motives, whereas dating is based on both sexual and emotional motives," says Mark. "When you're dating someone, you often enjoy spending time with the person outside of bed. But with a fling, you only spend time with someone outside of bed to get them into bed."

Flings can be a wonderful way to tide you over until a real date comes along. Or a nice distraction when the idea of a relationship is just too much to deal with.

"I was 20, she was in her 30s with three kids," says David, recalling one of his more memorable flings. "She hadn't been involved with anyone since her husband died three years earlier. She needed some male attention from someone who didn't demand too much, but who could be there whenever she wanted. The evening we met, we weren't exactly subtle about our needs and desires. She needed male companionship and I had an erection the size of Montreal. What followed was a fling in which I gave her companionship and my, uh, youthful enthusiasm. She, in turn, taught me how to please a woman. She was a good and patient teacher."

Handy things, flings.

# 8

# Don't Be Cruel

## The Art of Rejection

I saw rejection described somewhere once as "a partial death." A little melodramatic, perhaps, but not so far from the truth. A swift kick in the gut is probably a little closer to how it really feels.

When it comes to turning someone down, let's face it, there's really no nice way. Even if someone isn't wildly interested in you and is asking you out on a lark, turn 'em down, and it smarts. Maybe even more so in this case, since they didn't necessarily want to go out with you in the first place. And you turned them down. Double ow!

But while there is simply no way to make rejection feel good for the person being rejected (unless maybe the rejector walks out afterwards and gets hit by a bus), there is a better way to handle it than to say, "Eeew, I don't like you, go away."

When it comes to turning someone down, be gentle, but be honest. There's no need for bloodshed, but you also don't want to leave any scraps of hope for them to grasp onto either. Saying you're really busy for the next six months only prolongs the agony. They'll keep trying, no matter how many times you tell them you're going out of town to visit an old friend. Some people can't – or don't want to – take the hint.

If you do go out with someone only to realize you'd have been happier staying home sorting socks, you still have to at least pretend to be nice. After all, the person went to all that effort to show you a lousy time. Getting out of a date mid-way if it stinks is a bit tricky. Best to see it through and end it as quickly as possible with a "Thanks for a nice time. Bye." That's it, over, you're free. No "I'll call you sometime" (because you know you won't). No "Let's just be friends" (because if you don't want to be, you'll just have to ditch them as a friend later). No "I'm involved with someone else" (because you know they'll find out and think you're a fink and a liar). And just in case things get ugly, make sure you've got cab fare home.

If you really can't bear it and have to get out during the proceedings, I suppose you could feign illness or pretend you forgot to feed your fish. But that's a bit like trying to make your mom believe you're sick so you don't have to go to school. They know you're fakin'. You might as well face the music and be honest. Otherwise, you'll just have to set the record straight later when they call to see how you're feeling and ask you out again. Just try and be nice about it. The art of rejection is to keep all egos involved as intact as possible without insulting anyone's intelligence.

It's easiest if the feeling is obviously mutual. It's when you realize that one person wants to keep swimming and you're ready to get out of the pool that it can be icky. That's when you realize you have to have "the talk."

Keep it short, sweet and to the point. A bit like tearing off a Band-Aid: do it as fast and painlessly as possible. May I suggest something like "Look, you're a wonderful person, but the chemistry just isn't right" or "We simply have different interests" type-of-thing, as opposed to something like "Well, gee, you're butt ugly and I'm just not attracted to you." The idea is to be direct without getting personal. No need to tell the person they bore you to tears and have halitosis extraordinaire.

Limit the question period after. If the rejected party persists, just say "I'm sorry, that's how I feel." Elaborate explanations about how messed up you are, how bad you would be for them or how you're not ready for a relationship will just leave you both feeling rotten. It's bad enough getting rebuffed. Having to then watch the person flail about trying to explain themselves is salt in the wound.

"We were out at a bar and even the several Scotches I downed couldn't save the evening," Dawn recounts. "He was so obviously into it, but I was so not. At some point in the evening, I started to babble about how unsure I feel about men and relationships right now because I've had some pretty difficult experiences in the past two years, and how I was recently involved with someone and it was very intense and complicated and blah blah blah…Not only was this way too much information, it didn't even work. His response to me was, 'Okay, I can take it slowly.' Arghhhhhh."

Like I said, you have to be clear and, more important, to the point. And no backing down when they try to negotiate ("C'mon, just give me a chance. You'll see how great I am."). No matter how guilty you feel.

Sugar-coating a rejection with some lame explanation that probably isn't even true is just plain insulting. Saying something like, "I'm not ready to pursue something," is simply a way of saying, "I'm not ready to pursue something with you." Same goes for, "I'm too busy for a relationship." Like you wouldn't find the time if someone you couldn't resist showed up? It all adds up to the same thing: "I'm not interested in a relationship with you."

Besides, making up shit often backfires. Like saying you can't see someone because you have a terminal illness when you don't. "I went out with this guy who gave me the big brush-off by telling me he was dying of leukemia. I kid you not," Yves tells me. "Then I ran into him on the street like five years later."

That's always a fun one: running into people who have rejected you, especially if they told you they didn't want to get involved with anyone right now, and then you see them deep tongue-diving with someone else while you're walking down the street.

That's almost as bad as someone who strings you along because they're not ready to give you up, but they don't want to commit to anything either. They want to leave their options open. Understand this: People are not like furniture or clothing. You can't put them on hold while you consider whether or not you want to make the investment.

Some people save themselves the trouble of having to reject someone by simply avoiding the deed altogether. You know, not returning phone calls until the person finally gets the hint, or agreeing to go out and then not showing up. All evil, cowardly stuff.

### Date from Hell

I went out with this lawyer who I had a really big crush on. I asked him out and it was clearly meant as a date. When we were on the date I realized that he was kind of an asshole, and his way of indicating that he wasn't that interested in me was to say after dinner, "Let's go to a gay bar." At the bar he spent the whole night checking other guys out. It was a nasty experience.

As for the rejectee, unlike in the professional world, persistence will not pay off. Continuing to call will not make the person eventually come around. A big, shiny, "Oh well, too bad, your loss," is your best rejection comeback, delivered with a smile and one of those smart little laughs that look great in movies. You'll come off strong and confident. Who knows, maybe it'll even impress them enough to…Forget it, don't even think about it. Get out of there quick while your ego is still recognizable. You don't want a scenario like the one Amy endured.

"I was so crushed by this guy. We went out twice and then he told me he wasn't ready to pursue something right now. I had sensed this already but had hoped it wasn't so black and white. For some weird reason, being rejected by him only made me realize even more how much I liked him, and I was willing to be involved on any terms he set. I felt pretty pathetic."

Another word to the rejectee. If someone is telling you they're not ready to pursue something right now, as I said earlier, they are really saying they do not want to pursue something *with you*. No amount of crying or begging will change this. Save yourself the humiliation and walk away.

Although, I will admit, sometimes calling people on this kind of shit can be very empowering – if you can keep it together when you do it. Like if someone sleeps with you and then doesn't call you.

"I decided to call him, but I didn't want it to be too heavy, so I just said jokingly, 'Hey, are you blowing me off?'" says Jennifer. "He was taken aback that I would be so blunt about it and tried to play dumb, like, 'What do you mean?' So I repeated the question, because sometimes guys are kind of thick and don't get it the first time. He finally sort of admitted he was blowing me off and then launched into that 'I don't want to be in a relationship. I just wanted something casual' stuff. I said I thought we *were* being casual. He said, 'Casual to me does not include having sex.' So why the hell did he have sex with me, then? That crap drives me nuts."

Bottom line: be honest. Not brutally honest, but respectfully honest. You're not so special that he or she can't live without you. In fact, you'll be happy to know that unrequited love is no longer as great a cause for suicide as it once was. It hurts, but we survive. We may even get back on the horse and try again.

## Ouch!

Ah, but you folks out there are brutal. Here's what some of the people I spoke to have dished out and taken when it comes to rejection:

- "Sorry, I can't dance…I'm rolling a cigar."
- "I've physically turned my back on someone and started a conversation with someone else."
- "Thanks, but no thanks."
- "Get lost."
- "I was being pursued by this guy and then *he* turned *me* down when I finally agreed to go out with him."
- "Sorry, I can't get together today…I've got to wash my socks."
- "Sorry, my mother's having brain surgery."

## Top Ten Rejection Lines and What They Mean

1. I have a boyfriend/girlfriend. (Okay, so s/he's really my ex, but I'm too much of a coward to be honest with you, so I'm using them as an out.)

2. My life is too complicated right now. (And you're not interesting enough for me to want to accommodate.)

3. I don't date people I work with. (Well, not ones that work in your corner of the office, namely you.)

4. It's not you, it's me. (It's not me, it's you.)

5. I'm concentrating on my career. (Even something as boring and unfulfilling as my job is better than you.)

6. Let's be friends. (I could use you to give me a fresh perspective on problems I have with the men I do want to date.)

7. I'm not attracted to you in "that" way. (I'm not attracted to you, period.)

8. I think of you as a brother/sister. (You've got the sex appeal of a slug.)

9. You deserve better. (I'm a coward.)

10. I'm still getting over my last relationship and I'm not ready to see someone new. (I'm not attracted to you enough to get over my last relationship.)

# Keepin' Your Cool: Things Not to Do When Someone Rejects You

We've all had our moments of rejection hysteria. But we're grown-ups now, and there are things you really don't want to do when you're rejected. For example:

- Cry hysterically.

- Beg.

- Throw a fit.

- Throw a glass.

- Throw a tantrum.

- Throw all his clothes in a pile and set them on fire.

- Put sugar in his gas tank.

- Steal his phone book and call everyone in it and tell them he wets his bed.

- Plaster her picture around town with the caption: "This woman loves Michael Bolton."

- Leave a pet iguana on her doorstep.

## Oh Well, Your Loss:
## Snappy Comebacks to Nasty Rejection Lines

You may not get the same thrill saying these things as you might by setting his clothes on fire. However, coming up with a clever rebuttal when someone rejects you is almost as satisfying. Next time, try one of these.

**Rejection Line:** Let's be friends.
**Clever Comeback:** No thanks, I have lots of friends.

**RL:** I'm just not ready for a relationship right now.
**CC:** That's okay, I only wanted to have sex with you anyway. Too bad.

**RL:** I'm sorry, this just isn't working out.
**CC:** What isn't? Sorry, did you think this was a date?

**RL:** I'm not attracted to you.
**CC:** That's funny, I was about to tell you the same thing.

**RL:** You deserve better.
**CC:** Oh well, I guess I'll have to practise my tantric sex moves on the next guy.

**RL:** I just don't think I'm right for you.
**CC:** Oh, my roommate will be so disappointed. She's waiting for us to come home so we can all have sex together.

# Now What?
## Devising Your Follow-Up Plan

Suppose you do actually make it to and survive a first, um, non-date with someone. Now, lucky you gets to figure out if you want a second non-date with him or her. *Then* you get to sort out at what point it finally becomes – wait for it! – the *pièce de resistance*, a full-fledged "thing." Makes you just want to jump up and invite someone to a movie, don't it?

But hang on a second. I'm moving way too fast here. First things first. Let's step back to even before the first date for a moment, shall we? I've already talked about "sealing the deal" and how to conduct yourself on the actual date. But there are some potentially complicated matters that can arise between the time you actually meet someone and the date itself that deserve a little attention.

## Give Me a Call:
## How to Handle That First Phone Call

You've met someone, there seems to be a mutual interest, you get their number. Now what do you do? The follow-up to this moment is crucial.

I was at a party a while back, and I ran into a guy I'll call Bill. I'd had a bit of a thing for Bill back at school, but he had a girlfriend at the time so I got over it. This night, he was obviously single and so I was, albeit freshly so. Well, we hit it off and at the end of the night he told me to call him. Didn't give me his number, just said I should call him. We both knew I could easily get his number through the mutual friend who had invited us both to the party, which I promptly did, but then held off on using it. I'd been somewhat burned by my recent relationship and didn't want to get burned again, despite the obvious mutual attraction Bill and I had enjoyed at the party.

Then our mutual friend told me Bill had asked *him* for my number. I figured if Bill had gone to the trouble to get my number, he must still be interested, so he could call me. I never heard from him and put it out of my mind. Then, about a month later, I came across Bill's number and just decided to call. Bill wondered why I waited so long. He said he'd figured I wasn't interested. I told him I knew he had my number, so I thought he would call me if he was still interested. He said he only got my number because he knew our mutual friend would tell me he had asked for my number, and that was his way of letting me know he was still interested. He'd hoped that might make me call. Sheesh.

Confused? Tell me about it. Talk about lousy follow-up. No wonder it didn't work out. We couldn't even get it together at this crucial point in the game. And it is a bit of a game at this stage. All moves and countermoves.

Which brings me to the point of this tale. Even if one of you gets bold enough to actually hand over your number, there are plenty of things that may stop the other person from actually dialing it. The biggie is probably fear

– as in *fear* of rejection, *fear* of appearing over-eager, *fear* of the other person not remembering you, *fear* of not knowing what to say when you call and *fear* that they've reconsidered in the meantime and decided you're an idiot.

Then there's the question of how long to wait before you make the call. While I waited a month to call Bill, most of you seem to feel three days is the magic number – a happy medium, I suppose, between seeming too eager and not eager enough.

With all this stress surrounding one phone call, no wonder it's so much easier to say "screw it" than take the risk and call, especially if you weren't completely bowled-over to begin with.

So anyway, Day Three arrives, you pull the little crinkled piece of paper out of your pocket and hope it's still legible after pawing it for three days. You finally build up the courage to make the call, having practised a smart, brief, charming-but-to-the-point intro. Then you get the answering machine, which causes you to suddenly lose your composure and blather on incoherently for two minutes about how, "It was great to meet you, and I dunno, I just thought maybe, I dunno, if you had some time, that maybe, I dunno, we could go for coffee, but I understand if you're too busy…um, sorry…uhh…call me sometime."

You hang up in horror, racking your brain to come up with some possible way to erase your message when you realize you have to call back because you forgot to leave your number. Woohoo, ain't this fun?

Note: If you do leave a message and it isn't returned, you are allowed a second call (besides the call-back to leave your number). But that's it. One unreturned call could mean he or she didn't get the message or was out of town. A second unreturned call means you're being blown off.

Forget that "Rules" crap about not calling him or letting him call you until he gets you in person. If a guy calls you and leaves a message and you want to go out with him, call him back. Even if you don't want to go out with someone, it's a nice courtesy (and you'll score good karma points) to at least call them back and say, "Thanks, but I've thought about it and I don't think it would be a good idea." After all, you did give them your number in the first place.

I know, sometimes you give someone your number without really thinking about it or to be polite, or we let someone give us their number because it's what we think we should do. And then we regret it. For some guys, I think it's something of a prize to get a girl's number. It doesn't mean he has any intention of using it. That's a charming little game, though, isn't it?

If you want to be clear to someone that you want them to call you, lay it on a little thick when you give them your number. Press it meaningfully into their hand, look directly in their eyes and say with the utmost sincerity, "I really would like you to call me."

It will clear up any doubt on their part and make it easier for them to call if they're interested. And since you've been clear about the fact that you're interested, if they don't call, you know they're obviously not.

Then you give 'em hell next time you see them.

## When Sparks Fly: How to Proceed After a Successful First Date

Sex isn't the only time when women often take longer. A report in *Playboy* a few years back said women take up to an hour on a first date to decide if they're going to want a second date. Men apparently take only fifteen minutes to come to their conclusion.

Truth be told, I think this is being generous to both sexes. Again, just like a job interview, most of us often know within the first few minutes whether your date will make the shortlist. Sometimes you both come to the same conclusion and it's obvious. Suddenly, the bar is closing and you're both still yacking away, oblivious to everything around you. You float out the door together in search of the nearest all-night diner so you can continue the date.

And sometimes you think it's obvious, but you're wrong.

It's amazing how two people can go out on the same date and have such different experiences. Here you are, thinking the two of you are bonding as you spill your guts to him about your work, your relationship with your mother and your dog's bladder infection, when really he is simply too polite to object and let you know that he's ready to pummel you.

"I hate the feeling of uncertainty," says Walter. "When you're not sure the other person feels the same way, or could actually be completely bored and never wants to see your face again. And since she won't tell you honestly, you get to enjoy the suspense for a few days because she said, 'Well, thanks, I'll call you sometime.'"

Yes, it's true, women do it too.

There's probably nothing worse than thinking a date went well, having the person say they'll call you and then they don't. Please, for the sake of human kindness, if things don't work out and you're not planning on calling again, don't say you will. If you feel the need to say something at that awkward moment at the end of a not-so-successful date, "Thanks for the date. Good night," will do fine. Remember the rejection rules. Don't leave room for misinterpretation.

It may be a bit harsh, but it's better than a flippant "I'll call you" tossed at your date at the end of the night. That usually means he or she won't, but is too much of a coward to be honest about it. You don't want someone like that calling you back anyway, do you, even if you THINK you really like him or her. If you're left wondering whether the person is gonna call, they probably won't. You might as well wrap your mind around it now and avoid the calluses on your fingers you'd get from checking your messages 10 times a day.

If you do really want to see the person again, make it clear at the end of the date. "I had a really great time. I'd love to see you/call you again if that's okay with you," delivered while looking directly at them, will do the trick.

And then call. I'm a sucker for a guy who calls and thanks me for the date, yes, the very next day, especially if the feeling is mutual. Yikes!

In fact, if I had a good time, I may even be real bold and, goodness, call him and tell him so. It doesn't have to be a "Hey, that was a great date. Wanna meet my family next weekend?" kinda thank you. Just a "Hey, I had a good time last night. Thanks." Even if things don't work out, if it's true, what have you got to lose?

I think highly of a guy who is polite enough and appreciative enough to thank me after he's had a good time – so why wouldn't he feel the same? If he reads more into it, who cares, that's his problem. I figure, if you like someone, tell them. If they don't feel the same way, or are obviously not ready for anything more, better to find out now before wasting any more time. Honesty – what a novel idea, eh?

So why don't people do this? Part of it is that we worry that the other person will feel pressured or think we're more serious than perhaps we are. It's self-preservation. We're not about to put our egos on the line like that. Especially if we've been burned before by baring our souls too early.

So, even if the sparks were flying and we're almost sure the other person will want to see us again, we play the waiting game.

"I usually wait three days after the first date to call," says Mark. "That's the rule. One day is too anxious, but three days builds a little anticipation. Kinda like Christmas."

That magic number three again.

"I don't think I'd call the next day," adds Christine. "I'm usually pretty busy, so I won't call right away. Besides, I never know what to say."

Here, try this. Call the other person – yes, the very next day. Tell them that you enjoyed the date. See if they reciprocate. ("Me too" is usually a good sign.) Suggest another date. Wait for the answer. If the answer is positive, suggest something a bit different, maybe something a little more intimate, like a home-cooked meal, or maybe something more casual, like a party with friends. Ask if they have any suggestions. Wait for the answer. Make arrangements. Tell them you are looking forward to your date and say good-bye.

There now, that wasn't so hard, was it?

## Stoking the Fire: How to Proceed When Sparks Don't Fly but There's a Lukewarm Glow You'd Like to Explore Further

Dates don't always fall into the polar opposites of "sparks flew" or "no chemistry." Sometimes, you had an okay time, conversation may have run dry a few times, you were both nervous, but it wasn't disastrous. What do you do then?

"If I think she's worth it, I'd give it a second chance," says Tom. "I'd say, 'Look, I had a nice time, and I think maybe we should see each other again.' I wouldn't book something right on the spot, though. I'd play it safe. I'd say, 'Talk to you soon,' or something."

Hmm...With that kind of enthusiasm, I don't know that I'd want to give

Tom a second chance. I figure, either you want to see the person again or you don't. If you're unsure, you have to at least *act* enthusiastic. Otherwise it doesn't stand a chance. The worst you can lose is your pride if the other person is completely not into see-ing you again. That's when you tell them you were just try-ing to be nice.

"I recommend to people that, unless the person is just offensive to you in every way possible, to give somebody a second date," says Dr. Lila Gruzen. "It gives you a chance to see if they're any different the second time. Maybe they were just nervous on the first date, which happens to all of us. Then, on the second date, if you really cannot find any-thing in common, I would advise you to move on. If you do have something in com-mon, but you're still not sure, I would not be so quick to write people off because of one thing. You know, 'I really like him, but…he has an old junky car.' Because, you never know. You don't know about the future of this person, so why not give it a little bit of time and see. I don't think your time is so valuable that you can walk away from someone who could have been your best mate in the world. We can't afford to do that."

### Date from Hell

I'd met this woman a few times and there seemed to be some mutual interest. So one Friday night she called and invited me out for dessert. I thought she was cool, so I decid-ed to go. It was winter and my face was dry, so I put this moisturizer on that my mom had given me. I got to our meeting spot and it was this chi-chi kind of place. We started talking and I started sweating. Like really, really sweating. Eventually it got so bad that I had to excuse myself and I went and washed up. It was really embarrassing, and after-wards I thought, "Oooh, that was bad." But we ended up going out for three years and often laughed about that date. She's still con-vinced that I was just nervous, but I swear it was some weird reaction to that cream.

So, unless you're utterly appalled by them, it might not be a bad idea to give your date a second chance. After all, who is truly themselves on a first date? Someone who seems aloof and disinterested might really be painfully shy. Or someone who is overly chatty and overbearing may be overcompen-sating for their nervousness.

Sadly, it seems that we're often so terrified of getting closer to people or worried that they might think we're more interested than we are, that even the slightest doubt will stop us. When you think about it, how many of your friends did you connect with right off the bat? No doubt you grew to like many of them more over time. We're not so forgiving with potential relationships. If it's not all there and revealed in a three-hour date, we give up on it.

Like Karen. "It has to be there in the initial five minutes," she says. "For me, when I'm indecisive, it means no." Suit yourself, Karen, but I think you might be taking first impressions a little too seriously.

That's not to say that giving it more of a chance always works. Some people let things go on longer than they should. "I might continue to see a woman if she is really super-interested," says John. "I go along with it for a while, just to see if I will feel something deeper with time. Usually it doesn't happen and I regret having let things go on too long, allowing the woman to develop unrealistic expectations." And you to develop your ego.

I admit, though, it's hard to resist an ego stroke once in a while. "I like the fact that somebody thinks I'm Queen Hot Shit," says Tara. "I think it's flattering. Occasionally someone will think that I'm great and I realize that I want them to keep liking me. Even if I don't like them back. The attention and affection can be very seductive."

Having someone like you, even when you don't like them back, can be extremely validating. And we all like to be validated. Just remember, these are *people* you're dealing with here. They have feelings and need to be handled with care. They may think that liking you will be enough to make you eventually like them back. You're gonna have to break it to them eventually. Be nice. After all, they did give you an ego massage.

## Juggling Act: Keeping Your Options Open

Simply put, "multi-dating sucks," says Karen. "I hate feeling like I'm not good enough for this guy to stop shopping for a better catch."

Still, you have to admit, there are times in your life when you're just not ready to settle on one fish, but you're not ready to throw it back yet either.

When it comes to dating more than one person at a time (if you should be so lucky!), people are of mixed minds. As I mentioned in the discussion about rejection (Chapter 8, "Don't Be Cruel"), you don't want to string someone along for too long while you figure out what you want. But you don't necessarily want to turn your back on something before you're ready. It's a fine line and you have to be careful how you walk it. One thing is for sure, however, if you must juggle, discretion is advised.

"I'm okay with someone seeing more than one person at a time as long as they're not serious about one person in particular," says Sarah. "However, they shouldn't try to conceal what they're doing. There's no need to publicize it – just be open."

"Dating is fun, and the more the merrier," says Ann-Marie. "You learn a lot about yourself and others from dating. Just don't overbook. When love comes to town and you are serious about someone – then you don't want to be with anyone else. Until that happens, enjoy."

And make sure you have a good memory. "I've dated several people at once before, when I was younger," says Jeff. "But it's too hard to handle when it comes to remembering names, preferences, conversations, places, shared jokes and passions."

I can imagine. "Oh, honey, I loved the way you did that funny thing with your penis." "Um, I don't have a penis, dear." I see what ya mean there, John, uh, I mean, Jeff.

Some people just can't keep more than one ball in the air. "I found multiple dating stressful," says Amy. "And I hate fibbing even before there's any real commitment. And you HAVE to lie when you're dating more than one person. No guy I've ever met will date you if he thinks you're dating someone else, unless his ego is such that he thinks he can 'win you over.'"

But that doesn't mean that you need to make yourself completely available to anyone, especially early in the game. There's no harm in letting the other person realize you have your own life, and if that includes a few other interested parties – well, more power to you. Just be sure that if you do decide you want one party to become your "special guest," always be sure to give them VIP treatment.

## Great Expectations

Expectations are right up there with what to wear as one of the most stressful aspects of dating. The two of you may be similar in lots of other areas, but if you have different expectations it can cause all kinds of trouble.

As I've already mentioned, very few people are prepared to put their cards out on the table right away when it comes to this. Sometimes I think it would simplify things a lot if we could. At the beginning of the evening, you pull out a questionnaire and hand it to your date:

Choose one of the following:

a) I want a long-term relationship with someone who is honest, communicative and commitment-friendly.

b) I'm looking for a fuck-buddy, but one I can talk to.

c) I'm just looking for a good time.

I think you get better at this as you get older. You may not state it outright, but if you're looking for something serious and the other party is not, you're less likely to stick around for dessert. Or vice versa: if you're simply looking for a good time, you can save time, skip dinner and get straight to dessert.

Unfortunately, being honest about your expectations often freaks people out. Especially if you're a guy. If a guy feels a woman's expectations closing in, she's suddenly pressuring him, trying to nail him down. Of course, if he's really into her, he has no problem calling her up 16 times a day. A woman who does that gets labeled "psycho," while the guy is just "love-struck."

But the truth is, even if you think you know what you want and lay it on the table, there is no way of controlling exactly what will happen. You may set up expectations that you can't live up to or that may change and develop as you go.

And these days, with so many options out there, plenty of us — guys and girls — are not willing to commit to anything before we absolutely have to. What if something better comes along, right? So we dance around each other, playing it safe, keeping our emotional distance, protecting our interests and never revealing too much. Once you've had your heart smashed to bits once or twice, you get a little over-protective of that vital organ. You're not gonna let just anyone toy with it.

I don't think it's such a bad thing to be a little suspicious, and you certainly never want to assume more than you should. But sometimes we become the victims of our own skepticism. We're so protective, we don't let anyone in. And then we can't figure out why someone isn't responding to us in the way we'd like them to. If we were a little more up front about what we expected, we'd save ourselves a lot of trouble.

You know what I mean. He or she hasn't called you back after a date, although you're certain there was a mutual attraction. You concoct an entire scenario in your head for why they haven't called you. You check your messages compulsively, you wonder what's wrong with you, what's wrong with them. You finally can't take it anymore and call them, and they act completely normal. So you hold back your diatribe and mention in your most casual tone that you were surprised not to hear from them. You know, "I'd thought maybe the two of us could have done something this past weekend." They come back with a casual, "Oh, why didn't you call? I just assumed you were busy." Arghhh.

Of course, they could have called you. But they were no doubt too busy protecting themselves. Sometimes, it makes things a whole lot easier if you just speak your mind and face the consequences. Revealing your expectations doesn't mean you have to get them to sign a long-term commitment agreement on the first date. It just helps sometimes if you at least know whether you're on the same playing field. It can save a lot of time and agony. And you'd get to go out on the weekend instead of sitting home waiting for your phone to ring.

## Is This a "Thing" Yet?
## How to Tell When It's Official

I went out with this guy once and we were both determined to take things slowly. We kept telling people that we weren't in a "relationship." After about six months, our friends and family were giving us such a hard time about what we called our "situation," we decided to call it "Frank." We "Franked" for almost a year before we started to toy with the "R" word.

It's almost inevitable that if one date becomes two dates, then three, etc., the pressure to give it a name eventually arises. This is the tricky part, because of the expectations that go hand-in-hand with relationship titles. And while, yes, you do want to get a sense of what's happening between the two of you, you don't want to wreck it by naming it before the other person is ready.

A word of caution: while the whole "Rules" philosophy bugged my butt, the one thing I did agree with was the advice to take things slowly. Seeing someone you've just started dating more than once a week is pushing it. I honestly believe that. Even if the other person is calling you and wants to see you more often, don't. Make sure they know that you do want to see them, but this is the time to lay the groundwork for anything that may ensue. Plunging into it headfirst with both eyes closed will only backfire when you eventually want your life back. And you will.

And no use of the "L" word within the first six months. I mean it. Because no one can possibly "L" you in that short a time. For all their resistance to getting serious, guys are the worst for this. I've been with men who start throwing around "I love you's" within the first couple of weeks. I just say, "You can't love me. You don't even know me, you big, sappy romantic."

Obviously, what defines a "relationship" is unique to everyone. Sadly, at the same time that we are terrified to open ourselves up to someone, we are also anxious for the security of a "relationship." So we're more concerned about being able to *call* what we're in a "relationship" than we are about really putting in the time and effort to actually *make* it one. That is, taking things slowly and letting true commitment develop over time as you really get to know one another.

But hey, why make dinner when you can go to McDonald's?

# That Defining Moment

Here's how some of the people I spoke to defined the moment when dating becomes a "relationship":

- "You are on your way to being exclusive and you both want it that way."

- "Mutual commitment to each other — and communicating that!"

- "This may seem silly, but I like to verbally confirm our status if I think we have one: 'So, honey, are we official now?' Cheesy, but it saves much confusion and heartache, since you both know where you stand."

- "You know the other's faults like you know your own and are able to accept them."

- "When 'I love you's' have been exchanged. Just words, I know, but nice to hear." (Just remember what I said about the "L" word.)

- "When you can't stop thinking about the other person and it's reciprocated. At this stage, the perma-grin and that glazed look in your eyes often give it away."

- "When your plans with him or her come first and foremost before others. When you've invested enough of yourself to be hurt if anything were to change."

- "When you start doing the 'little' things together, like spending a Saturday morning drinking *café au lait,* doing crosswords, going grocery shopping…Stuff like that."

- "The 'parent test' is a major sign. That is, when one of you invites the other into the family home for dinner."

- "Unfortunately, in most cases, I'd have to say that dating becomes a 'relationship' when the guy wants it to."

- "When you start to feel trapped. (I'm not a big fan of relationships at this point, you might notice.)"

- "When you can sleep over when you have your period."

# 10

# Desperately Seeking, Um...
## Just What the Hell Are We Looking for Anyway?

I've heard it over and over again in my discussions with people about dating. "It's not that it's so hard to meet people, it's just hard to meet the *right* people." No wonder, given our expectations.

There was a day when you were lucky if you even scored basic compatibility in a partner, never mind love. Up until about the 18th century, marriage was more of a financial arrangement than anything else. All that other mushy stuff just got in the way. Even at the end of the 18th century, expectations in a partner were more practical than emotional. Consider this list of what men should look for in a woman, quoted by E. S. Turner in *A History of Courting*. The list first appeared in a book by William Cobbett called *Advice to Young Men*. Topping it, in the No. 1 spot, is...chastity! Yup, in those days, virginity was highly prized. In second place was piety, followed by industry, frugality, knowledge of domestic affairs, good temper and, finally, beauty.

Cobbett would be floored by what most of us modern folk are looking for in a mate. These days, we head out on a date fully armed with a mental checklist of emotional, physical and intellectual expectations that would make Mr. Cobbett seem easy to please.

For example, here's what it would take for Steve, a 29-year-old playwright I met in a bar one night: "Musical taste, intelligence, education, independence, life experience, maturity, creativity, passion, open-mindedness, loves the arts, likes to party and is fairly attractive and slim." And for dessert?

## Gender Equality: Are Men and Women Looking for the Same Things?

I asked straight men and women what they thought the opposite sex considers to be the perfect type. The men described what they thought of as women's ideal type as something like this: "Over six feet, toned body, relatively large penis, financially successful, charming, intelligent, a great sense of humor."

The women figured most men's ideal type as: "Blond, big breasts, small waist, perfect body and naturally beautiful (as in, no Tammy-Faye makeup.)"

This backs up what the folks in the lab coats say: Men focus on looks and women focus on money and intelligence. It's biological, they insist. Men are just looking for good specimens for their seed and women are looking for reliable daddies for their kids. More on that in the next chapter, but for now, listen up!

While there's some truth to these stereotypes, I'm happy to say that our intellect seems to have butted into the evolutionary process at some point, because from where I sit, what men and women want is not so clearly divided. Our mental checklists actually carry many of the same items. Maybe not in the same order and maybe not always expressed in exactly the same way, but they're not as different as we sometimes like to think.

Basically, we all want someone who looks half decent, has half a brain and can make us laugh. We want someone who appreciates us and who has enough confidence in themselves so that we can appreciate them. We wanna communicate, connect and turn each other's cranks. Sometimes we just want sex, sometimes we want a relationship.

Most of the people I spoke with said they don't have an ideal type. "The people I've dated are all different – different heights, different weights," says Amy. "I can't say I have a type."

Even if we do have an ideal type, the people we date don't always match it. I still have an absolute knee-jerk reaction to tall, lanky redheads, but I hardly ever seem to date any. Maybe that's because the two I did date broke my heart to smithereens. But I digress.

"I used to think there was a type that I liked," says Alex. "Back then, if you were unusual, strange and appalling in some way, then I was interested. Now I try to be more focused on the individual. What can I learn from you? That's more what's on my mind."

We're not all so tolerant.

Even if we don't have an ideal type, most of us have some pretty specific ideas about what we're looking for. Some of these ideas can be considered gender-specific, some have developed through years of experience and some are just downright shallow.

## Makin' a List:
## What Are Your Mate Requirements?

Speaking of shallow, yes, let's face it, looks matter. Mark puts it this way: "As a first impression, what else are you gonna look for? You gotta have a reason to find out about the person."

Obviously, we're a little more honest than they were in William Cobbett's day. In fact, looks has scooted right up to No. 1 for lots of guys. As our resident singles expert, Rich Gosse of American Singles, says, "The first three items on every man's list are the same: Looks, looks and looks."

Like I said, there is obviously some truth to the stereotypes. "I'll be honest with you," says Martin. "I wish I could tell you it was the quiet, intelligent women that I was attracted to. But the number-one thing that attracts me is the physical. It starts with the face, then the body, then the way she's dressed. It'd be great to say it's the other stuff, but it's not. Physical first, and the rest is secondary."

"A woman's beauty is important," says Tom. "But it's the eyes that just take me out."

At least he's being a little more politically sensitive about it and opting for safer body parts. Then again, as Martin says, "What am I gonna say? 'Wow, look at that woman across the street, what great eyes.'" He admits that for him, it's all about her physical beauty and the way she carries it.

Of course, it's all about personality for us, right girls?

"That's bullshit," says Rich Gosse. "Basically, women are looking for one of two things, and preferably both things. Looks and money."

We're so much deeper, we women.

"Yeah, right," Gosse continues. "Women are just as superficial about men, they just have a different list. For men it's all about how she looks. For women, he's gotta have looks or he's gotta have bucks or both. I tell men that if you want to attract a woman, you have to look like Tom Selleck or your bank account has to look like Tom Selleck."

Yech, Tom Selleck? Never mind, what if he doesn't have looks or bucks?

"Then he'd better settle for a woman who doesn't look too good. Because good-looking women are either going to marry men who look good or whose bank accounts look good."

I dunno, maybe blame it on the economy. Either that or all the women I spoke to are ugly, since most of them hadn't found themselves in this dilemma.

"Women will choose character over money every time," Amy says. And she's a gorgeous chick! See how sincere we are? "And a developed upper body," she adds.

Okay, so we can be just as bad. "My first thought when I see a man is, 'Do I want to have sex with him?'" admits Ann-Marie.

As for me, short guys just don't do it. It's not my fault, really. Just look around you. How many dime novels have the heroine "gazing *down* into his eyes?" Ads for movies and the front covers of Harlequin romances never have the girl locked in the embrace of some studly guy who only comes up to her armpits. I ain't sayin' it's right, I just fell for the social conditioning. Not all women feel the same way, honest, guys.

### Date from Hell

I was working at a bookstore and this girl used to come in all the time. I remember liking her because she sat on the floor reading astrology books. She was very into astrology and we would talk about it sometimes. One day I asked her if she would like to go for dinner. We ended up going to a cafe and she was very distracted. I ordered a meal and she, like, ordered a salad. Then, while I was eating my dinner, she said, "Do you mind if I smoke?" I said, "Uh, no." Next thing I knew she said she needed a match and left. That was the end of the date.

Thankfully, even though we all may admit looks are important, most of us at least still manage to have some form of individual taste when it comes to what we find physically appealing. And most of us also know that physical appearance can be deceiving. Beauty is only skin deep and all that. It's what gives all us ordinary-looking folks a chance.

"In the initial stages of meeting someone you may think, 'Oooh, you're really cute, I have to talk to you,'" says Sarah. "But what comes out of their mouth when you talk to them can either make them more attractive or make you suddenly have somewhere else really important that you have to be."

I think the importance of looks also lessens as you get older, which is convenient, since that's when your own looks start to, ahem, mature, and "You look good" becomes "You look good for your age."

"Looks are important," says Walter. "But, especially as I get older, they're not paramount. They're not the first thing. Whereas they might have been before."

So after looks, what's important?

"Single's good!" laughs Karen.

"Humor, hands down, every time," says Dawn. "If you're funny, I'm yours. I always fall hard for the guys that make me laugh."

"The entertainment factor has to be high because I can amuse myself for months," says Lise. "Besides, if you're funny, you are by definition smart."

"I know some funny assholes," Alex argues.

"Well, they've gotta be funny but there's gotta be something else there that you can talk about," Lise explains. "You want a guy who can hold a conversation but who's not too serious or boring. You need the humor."

Funny, but humor didn't make it on a lot of male lists (although one guy said he likes a woman who laughs at his jokes. Does that count?). But intelligence did.

"For me, it's 'Is she smart?'" says Tony. "Does she know what she's talking about? Or is she always worried about her hair?"

A study in the U.S. asked women and men how intelligent their date would have to be for them to consider having sex with them. Women said the man had to be markedly above average in intelligence for her to sleep with him, and men said the woman had to be markedly below. When it comes to casual sex for men, the study concluded, intelligence plays less of a role. But in a long-term partner, intelligence was very important for both men and women.

Hmm...If you want to get laid ladies, play dumb, I guess. And guys, be on your toes.

So what about age? A lot of women in their 30s that I spoke to have struck younger men off their list.

"I made a rule that I'll never date anyone younger than me again," says Karen. "Not radically younger anyway. I've had too many bad experiences with really immature guys. Guys who were too young to know what they wanted, who weren't over themselves yet. It was too hard watching them go through things that I've already gone through."

Men, on the other hand, have few objections to dating younger women. Particularly as they get older. I guess having a good-looking younger woman on your arm makes you feel good about yourself. Like you've still got it.

Of course, we all want someone who makes us feel good about ourselves. For some reason women have a harder time finding this. We seem to be better at finding guys who make us feel shitty about ourselves. A lot of women still don't feel they deserve to be worshipped as much as guys, I guess. Maybe it's because men are more used to having their egos fed on a regular basis. Particularly by the women they are making feel shitty.

"I'm really looking for somebody who thinks I'm totally amazing," says

Jennifer. "I find that often, when I go out with a guy, I spend too much time thinking, 'Do they like me? Do they like me?' I want to have a sense that they think I am the best thing that ever happened to them. That they are thankful that they have me in their life. And I want to feel the same way about them."

"I want someone who's happy with their own life but who's obviously into me," says John. "To be with someone who clearly thinks you're totally wonderful, that's really seductive. And as she learns about your quirks, she thinks they're wonderful too. I'm a complete sucker for that."

Of course, if you don't think his quirky way of not calling you is so wonderful, don't pretend it is.

Which brings us to honesty.

"Honesty and a sense of integrity" are high on Walter's wish-list. "I like women who are committed to honest communication. Who are interested in having relationships that are not all foggy and fucked up."

Then there's all the gushy hearts-and-flowers stuff – and it's not just girls who go for this. "I like good old-fashioned romance," says Sam. "It's not that I don't want some good old-fashioned hard sex once in a while, but I want something else too. I don't think that any guy has brought me flowers, but boy, that would make an impression."

Self-confidence is another biggie. "I want a guy who knows who he is and is comfortable with himself," says Ann-Marie. "You don't want anyone pathetic."

But not too cocky either. "I really like a man who's sure of himself, but not arrogant," says Jennifer. "I want him to be emotional. But I don't necessarily want him to put his head in my lap and cry."

Right. Basically we want 'em vulnerable but strong, sensitive but not falling apart. Men also like women who have their shit together.

"I like a woman who's not afraid to put me in my place when I'm out of line," says Mark. "A woman who doesn't want to be a doormat."

"I like a guy who's got the confidence to call me on some things," says Christine. "But who's sensitive enough not to be a jerk."

But of course.

## Checkin' It Twice

The people I spoke to who run matchmaking organizations say that when people sign up with these services, they are often required to come up with a list of what they're looking for.

Susan Mills of Executive Connections, a matchmaking service for well-heeled businesspeople in the U.S., says that in many cases this list is at odds with what the person says they need or want when she sits them down for a one-on-one interview. "I will often set them up with someone who doesn't necessarily match their original list, and they end up getting along great," says Mills.

In other words, maybe some of us need to rethink our lists. Rich Gosse offers his advice on how to revise your partner wish-list:

"I have people write down everything they could possibly fantasize about an ideal romantic partner. And once they have that all down, I have them go through that list and whittle it down to what I call a non-negotiable list, where they eliminate all the non-essentials.

"Then I tell them to go through each of the items on the list and ask themselves, 'If I met someone who was missing this quality, would I rather be single for the rest of my life than marry this person?' If the answer is 'no,' then cross it off the list. The non-negotiable list ends up being a real short, hard-core list of qualities. Possible candidates have to have every single one of these qualities. Otherwise, they don't even get your phone number."

So, you might consider giving some of the dates who don't measure up to everything on your initial 300-item list more of a chance. Like I said back in Chapter 5 ("How to Make an Impression"), while it's important to have standards when you go out on a date, you don't want to make your date feel like a lab rat that you're dissecting to see if all the parts are there. Once you've got your list down to the essentials, memorize it and then leave it at home.

# The Bare Essentials

Here are the most important items on the partner wish-lists of some of the people I spoke to. (I think some of them could still stand to lose an item or two.)

- Ambitious
- Can dance
- Enjoys life
- Generous
- Doesn't require mothering
- Doesn't like New Age music
- Frank
- Finishes their meal
- Isn't anal about cleanliness
- Sociable
- Isn't always in performance mode
- Secure
- Not too perky
- Carries themselves well
- Will give me their phone number easily

- Has a brain
- Doesn't own potpourri
- Smart, cute, funny, in that order
- Not living with their ex
- Politically compatible
- Optimistic
- Doesn't chew with their mouth open
- Honest
- Likes pets
- Doesn't like pets
- Doesn't own stuffed animals
- Sincere
- Isn't passive-aggressive
- Flexible
- Drives a stick-shift
- Easygoing

## Why Can't We Find It?

My mother would say we're too picky (but she married the first guy she ever dated). People often accuse us of being super-selective if we're less than snappy about getting ourselves hitched. More so, it seems, if you're a woman. You don't see a lot of films about guys facing the worst crisis of their life because they're 30 and unmarried. C'mon Hollywood, enough with that already! But yes, guys also get accused of being too picky.

"It's an absurd comment," complains Mark. "I simply know what I want."

Some of us have just raised our standards. "I'm in my 30s and I think I'm at a point where I've dated enough people to know what I like and what I don't like," says Ann-Marie. "If not wanting to waste my time on people I know I don't want to spend my time with makes me picky, I guess I'm guilty."

"It used to be that anybody with a pulse could ask me out and I'd say yes," says Sarah. "Now you've gotta have a pulse but you've also gotta have some other stuff going on."

I'm the first to admit, however, that sometimes what we think we want isn't necessarily the best thing for us. Witness women who go out with assholes. More on that baffling phenomenon later.

"I sort of know what I want, but I don't trust my judgment as much with relationships as I do with friendships," says Christine. "I'll meet someone and think, 'Oh, this is what I want,' but then I have to ask myself, 'Okay, is it just because this person is completely sexy to me, or do I actually think this is a nice person?' I'm getting better at hearing the warning bells in my head."

Sometimes the chemistry is stronger than we are. "I'm starting to trust that immediate chemistry less," says Nathan. "If I find myself thinking, 'Wow, we have all this chemistry,' I say to myself, 'Wait a minute, this is the same chemistry I had with the last person I went out with, and that was a terrible relationship.'"

The problem is, that kind of immediate chemistry is like a drug. And it can be habit-forming. Having been hooked a few times myself, I know how hard it is to kick. Why settle for something as boring as compatibility when you can get sucked into that exciting hormonal and emotional vortex instead? What can I say, we're addicted to drama. Blame it on the movies.

"If there's no drama, my fear is that things will be boring and predictable," says Lise.

"It makes you feel alive. And if there's not a lot of other stuff going on in your life, drama can be really addictive that way," says Mark.

But you gotta admit, all that excitement can get a bit tiresome after a while. "I'm bored with drama," Yves says. "I went out with this guy last summer who was such a drama queen, and really, it's irritating."

Some people have a harder time finding what they want because they haven't found themselves yet. Why deal with your own shit when you can find someone to date and foist it on them instead?

## The C-Word

Fear of commitment is one of the things women complain about all the time. "Guys just don't want to commit to a relationship," we whine. Of course, as Martin said to me, "It's not that men fear commitment. Usually when a woman accuses me of fear of commitment, it's often quite simply that I have a fear of commitment to her in particular."

Very funny, Martin. He was being a smart-ass when he said this, but I think there's some truth to it. A lot of guys think that it's a matter of finding the right person, then commitment and intimacy will automatically follow. They don't see it as something you have to work at.

Unfortunately, if you want to achieve true intimacy you have to work to achieve it. And that takes a real commitment.

"I think my number-one criterion in a man is that he should have an active interest in making a good relationship work," says Karen, "and not just some half-assed, 'if it gets too hard I quit' attitude.

"I want him to be thinking about how we can make things better. How are we not communicating? What's happening that's blocking our ability to have a better relationship? The problem is that the few of these men that are out there are usually already in good relationships."

But let's face it, for plenty of women, even if we did find one of these magical men, would we really know what to do with him? "I think my own fears can kick in when I meet someone who is truly great," admits Dawn. "I meet a fabulous, great, amazing guy and I start looking for the booby trap, the things I'm sure are wrong with him."

What can I say? Maybe we're so used to the challenge, it's no fun if it's too easy. John agrees. "I think a myth has been created around the idea that women are much more devoted to the concept of commitment than men are," he says. "Women play up that traditional role a little bit. It's a great way to divert attention from their own brand of commitment-phobia. In a lot of cases, if they were actually with a man who would give in the way they want, they would tend to run."

(Is *that* why we like jerks who treat us badly? Hey, give me a minute, I'm getting to that.)

Commitment is scary, for men or women. But that's because the only thing more frightening that making a commitment to someone is having them not return the favor, leaving your sorry ass rejected and alone.

Many of us will take anything that comes along to avoid being alone. The opposite to the commitment-phobe is the serial monogamist, who might never be satisfied, but never spends a Saturday night alone. They'll commit to something they don't even necessarily want just to avoid being single. Who cares if you're compatible?

Some people want to be loved so badly, they forget to even think about what they want themselves. "A lot of the times, it's more about getting a person to feel love for me," says Elaine, a 27-year-old daycare worker. "How I actually feel about the other person isn't an issue."

It's hard to find what you're looking for when you're too busy getting involved with anyone who'll like you.

This is not to say we're all needy, emotionally retarded basket-cases afraid to go after what we want. Some of us are just plain holding out until we find what we're after. Even if you're not exactly sure what that is. If that's being picky, than so be it. I like to think of it as having discriminating tastes. You're not about to settle for something mediocre. And that should be applauded.

"I don't want to make the same mistakes my mother did," says Karen. "She's on her third marriage and she's ended up in all these unhealthy involvements. I don't want to do that. I don't want to get divorced and I won't compromise the way she has."

Go girl. You just might want to check once in a while that your desire not to compromise isn't cleverly disguised as full resistance.

# What's Love Got to Do with It?

Part of the reason some of us struggle so much to find Mr. or Ms. Right is that we are looking for a magical thing called love. We expect love to smack us over the head immediately when we meet someone and then expect everything else to fall into place afterwards. Love conquers all, right? Dr. Lila Gruzen thinks we need to come off our romantic high horses and get real.

J: Are we looking for the right things in people?

L: No. I would love it if people would look for people who are great friends. You know, good friends to other people, good friends to themselves. Someone who could be a good friend to you. I think that most people are looking for that thrilling feeling. They want their heart to flutter when they kiss. I think they're looking for that drug called "love," and I don't think love is the most important thing in a relationship. At all.

J: Ack! No love. You mean our ancestors had it right? C'mon. You gotta have love.

L: I think commitment is much more important than love.

J: What's the difference?

L: Well, commitment means, "We stick this out no matter what, and do whatever we have to do to continue to grow and to make it better, and we both work at it, all the time."

J: But surely you have to have love for the person in order to be able to that?

L: Oh, not at all. When you personally make a commitment, there are times you don't want to be in that commitment. It doesn't matter what you commit to. Through my 11 years of college, I certainly didn't feel love for it. Sometimes I did, sometimes I didn't. Sometimes I didn't want to go to school another day, but I was committed to it.

J: But that was school. We're talking about people. Doesn't there have to be something there in the first place? Otherwise you might as well just pair people off and say, "Okay, you two, go on and make it work."

L: I'm talking about an established relationship. In an established relationship, commitment is much more important than love, because I think love comes and goes.

J: Do you think we've lost sight of the commitment aspect of relationships a bit? Because even though my parents didn't have all the things I might demand in a relationship now, the one thing that I did see about their relationship was that, no matter what, they just knew that they had to stick it out together. And that was a product of their times.

L: That's right. And short of abuse, I think that it's really urgent that people get back to that kind of thinking.

J: Well, when did it change? Where did we lose that?

L: I think that society just got more disposable in general. Now, when things don't work, we just throw them away. And love is not enough to sustain a relationship long term. Love fluctuates. Commitment doesn't.

J: You've been quoted as saying that "Love at first sight is nonsense."

L: That's right. Completely ridiculous. It's not possible.

J: So why do you think people believe in it?

L: Well, they want to believe in magic, in romance.

J: And you don't believe that there can be a chemistry that happens between two people when they first meet that says, "Okay. This is the person for me."

L: No. No. No.

J: As in, never.

L: Never. I think that you can be attracted to someone. I think you can lust for someone on your first meeting, but I think that the kind of love and commitment that lasts a lifetime needs a lot of time to grow and be nurtured.

## What Is It About Bad Boys?

Okay, so many guys have asked about this that I feel the need to explain ourselves. Why are women so insistent on going out with jerks?

"I have a friend who is a doctor," one guy wrote. "She teaches med students and worked her way through pre-med and Yale med school with no help from anyone. She has one small weakness: if you sent a decent guy and a creep to walk down that girl's street, she will find the creep and get involved with him."

It's true. For all our talk about wanting guys to be sensitive, we keep going out with the assholes. Nice guys can't figure out whether to be themselves or assholes to get a date, because when they don't treat us like shit, we just want to be their friends.

So, what is it about bad boys? "It's the thrill," says Tara. "If they drive motorcycles, play in a band or basically have no sense of responsibility, I'm in there. I'm my own worst enemy, really."

But what exactly is the thrill? "Danger." But why is danger such an attraction?

"Why do people race cars? It's the thrill of feeling very alive. Feeling like you're walking a tightrope with this person," Tara says.

"A friend of mine was dating a guy who was just too nice, just way too nice," Sarah tells me. "She said she wanted to puke, he was so nice. I asked her if she preferred him to be an asshole. She answers, 'Well, not an asshole, but just a little, you know, mad, bad and dangerous to know.'"

Take heart there, boys, we're obviously trying to figure out our bad-boy problem as well. Unfortunately, while we're getting past the denial, I think some of us are still stuck in the rationalization phase. Although our friend Lise has quite a developed philosophy on the bad-boy phenomenon.

"It's so much easier, on the surface, to connect with the young, fast boys," she explains. "I gravitate toward them in part because they are so utterly unsuitable for relationships. And there is a part of me, for all that I say I want to be in a relationship, that is truly afraid of what that really means. It means sharing your life, doing the laundry, never having the possibility of someone else's body in your arms. It means knowing someone has pimples on their bum, their breath in the morning is foul, their taste in shirts is terrible.

"It means being bored sometimes. And I hate being bored. I want to be comfortable, but not bored. And I'm not sure that exists. So I go for the thrill instead."

That also explains why we so often swing back and forth between boys who make us feel safe and in control, and those who make us feel out of control but thrilled. Consider it the female version of commitment-phobia.

The other thing that gets us is that, on some level, even though we know these type of guys are really bad news, we latch on to this naive belief that we'll be the one to turn them around. You know, "The love of a good woman."

We're trying to grow out of it.

"I think what I need is someone who used to be dangerous and is now trying to work on it," says Tara.

"I have this theory called 'The Dead Zone,'" says Jennifer. "There are all these women who are attracted to actors, musicians and guys with motorbikes because they're dangerous, they're gorgeous, they're fun, they're exciting – but they generally end up treating these women like crap.

"So these women eventually learn not to go after these kinds of guys anymore. Even if you feel the pull, you know where it will get you, so you don't go there.

"But the problem is, these women still haven't yet shifted into the phase where they're actually attracted to nice guys. So they're in 'The Dead Zone.' They won't go out with the bad guys, but somehow they're not feeling really excited about the nice guys. I'm sort of moving out of 'The Dead Zone' myself right now, finding nice guys more exciting. I'm starting to get there."

So all you "nice" guys, don't give up. But take this word of advice. Nice does not mean you'll put up with any shit we fork over. Nice means respect, respect for yourself and respect for her.

Hey, and if you've got a motorcycle, it might not hurt.

## "The One": Why Do Guys Expect to Find a Beautiful Princess?

"I gave up searching for the perfect woman. I kept finding her too often," Martin laughs.

If women have a complex about "bad boys," I think guys have a thing about "the one" that personally drives me a little nuts.

Despite the fact that women are always perceived as the sappy, romantic ones, I think guys are worse for thinking that one day, this wonderful, special woman will suddenly appear like a vision and he'll know immediately that she's "the one."

In the meantime, he'll fuck his brains out with every girl who isn't "the one."

Sure, women have their dreams of the knight in shining armor, but I can't help but think we're more willing to spend some time polishing his suit rather than waiting till a perfectly shiny one comes along to sweep us off our feet.

"I agree with that," says Sarah. "I was involved with this guy and he kept saying, 'I don't know, I care for you, I feel affection for you, but this doesn't feel right, it just doesn't feel right.' So we broke up and I saw him a few weeks later and he says, 'Oh, I started seeing somebody.' A month later she was pregnant. It was that fast. For him I guess, she was 'the one.'"

"This guy told me once that he has to be tricked into a relationship," says Ann-Marie. "And I've heard that before from men. It's as if they feel that something has to happen to them that they can't fight. For me, I've always wanted to be in a relationship where it's a choice. I want you to choose me. I don't want you to feel like I tricked you."

We all want to be swept off our feet by someone. But eventually, I think we have to come to terms with the fact that the ones who sweep us off our feet often end up dropping us at some point. Maybe because women have experienced this more (because we go out with so many jerks), we're more ready to give up on the concept of "the one."

"I used to think there was one soul-mate for me, like in a village in Africa maybe," says Jennifer. "That 'my' person existed somewhere on the planet. I've changed that a bit. I'd say there's maybe even four or five people who are the person for you.

"Two of them you'll never meet, one is already married, another is gay and the last one just broke up with someone and doesn't want to get involved right now."

Okay, some of us have given up on the idea a little more than others. Most of us have just gotten a little more realistic.

"I really don't buy into the notion that there's one or even 10 right people for you," says Ann-Marie. "I think that's a load of bullshit that we are sold in this culture. I think you make your own happiness.

"I just believe that everyone has redeeming qualities and you have to find them. You have to do something to make it happen. I'd love to find a great job, but I won't just stumble into it."

But people (and yes, I think men often more than women) do expect it to happen magically. They expect this total, fantastic experience to come along. Relationships aren't necessarily like that. Sometimes there is no white knight or beautiful princess, but people waste their whole lives waiting or not getting involved with anyone because they might miss their dream date when they magically appear on their doorstep.

Hopefully, they won't be out at the time.

## Popping the Marriage Question

The whole reason dating was created in the first place was to find yourself a marriage partner. But these days, marriage isn't quite the achievement it once was. People date to find a soul mate, someone to get through life with.

Sure, lots of people still believe in marriage, but more and more of you are questioning it. In fact, given the number of "Forget it," "Never" and "What for?" votes I received against marriage, plenty of you have downright rejected it.

"Marriage is bad. That was the first thing my dad told me," says Martin. "Don't ever get married."

Not all of you are so down on it, but I'm glad to see its appeal has definitely shifted in nature. For some, it's still about God and little pieces of stale cake. But for others, it's a really fun way to publicly announce you're crazy about someone.

"It's such a blast, getting married," says 31-year-old Tim, who recently married his girlfriend after living with her for four years. "Committing to your community and having your community support you: it's a wonderful public affirmation of your commitment. 'You're our friends, you're our community, and we love you. And you love us.' It's a gas."

Just don't make me wear the frilly white dress.

Sadly, however, sometimes marriage gets used for all the wrong reasons.

"My ex said if I'd married him he would have tried harder to make the relationship work," says Sandra. "I thought that was the biggest cop-out I'd ever heard. I mean, we were living together for four years and, in his mind, because I didn't want to get married, that proved I wasn't committed to the relationship."

Then there are those who are concerned that we don't take marriage seriously enough.

"I just believe that when you get married you should be sure that you're gonna spend the rest of your life with this person," says Tom. "People take that way too lightly these days. They get engaged like after a week."

Amy shares this view. "I'll get married when I know I want to spend the rest of my life with this person," she says. "If I know I want to have kids with this person. My cousin just got married, and she'd been with this guy only three months. They may be very happy, but there's also a huge chance that they won't. I say, why rush it?"

Then there's Walter, who says: "If you're living together for a long time, you might as well get married. I guess I'm old-fashioned that way."

I think it's cool if you want to make a public commitment to someone. I think it's wonderful to want to share your life with someone you love. I just think you shouldn't have to feel like a relationship is only legitimate when you both have a ring on your finger.

Then again, there are other considerations. As Eve pointed out, "If your boyfriend has dental care…"

But in the end, dating should not be about marriage (or dental care). If you're dating to find a husband or a wife, I think you're asking for trouble. You should be dating to find yourself a good, solid partner whom you can support, commit to, work through problems with and have fun with. Once you've got all that in place, then and only then can you start arguing about whether you should get married or not.

## The Single Life: Making the Best of It

In colonial times, the need for population was so great that bachelors were harassed and fined for being single. Sometimes they were even run out of town.

You could safely say that staying single has never exactly been embraced in our culture.

It's too bad, because there are great things about being single: the personal freedom, the independence, being able to hog the whole bed, bitching with all your other single friends about everything that's wrong with couples.

Yeah, there are lousy things too: the loneliness, constantly having to entertain yourself, having no one to scratch your back, the milk in the fridge going sour.

But there are pros and cons about being in a relationship too. The problem is, while we can often understand someone choosing to be in a lousy relationship, we can't seem to believe that anyone would choose to be single. Instead, we view it as a personal failure or an affliction. At best, we see it as a transient, semi-permanent state – a stopover until someone comes along. Sure it is. But if you treat it that way, you miss out on all the fun.

My friend Li said to me once, when she was trying to convince herself that her single status was a good thing, "The happy single person enjoys life and seeks someone to enjoy it with, while the unhappy single person seeks someone to make him or her happy."

Which doesn't mean that if you're single, you shouldn't let someone make you happy once in a while. The occasional romp is always a good mood booster. No one said you had to be celibate as well as single. There's just no need to foist yourself on the first person that looks twice at you.

Sure, some people stay single to avoid relationships. They're the ones that are always saying they don't "need" a relationship, as if they're trying to convince themselves more than you. We know that old trick. If you don't go near the stove, you won't get burned. But you could freeze your butt too.

There is a certain amount of bullshit you save yourself from by staying single. You don't have to worry about him calling, or whether she likes you or not. You can spend the energy on other things.

"It can be a lot of fun to be in a couple, and to wallow in all those wonderful gooey feelings," says Yves. "But there are times when going out with someone is just a really nasty distraction. Especially if it doesn't come to anything, you feel like, 'Shit, I've wasted all this time and energy thinking about this guy and what I'm gonna wear and what he thinks of me.'

Sometimes I just don't want to deal with it. I'd rather be alone."

Singlehood can be a good time to get to know yourself and your needs better. I tell ya, there's plenty of folks out there who could use a little stint of it.

"I have so many friends who are serial daters or serial monogamists," says Christine. "And it's painful to watch, because they make the same friggin' mistakes in every relationship they get into. I just want to scream at them, 'Try staying single for a while!'"

In fact, as Rich Gosse so aptly puts it, "The secret to being happily married is to be happily single first. If you're unhappily single, I can guarantee you'll eventually be unhappily married. You're gonna lower your standards and marry someone who is inappropriate for you.

"On the other hand, if you're happily single, you're gonna stay single until you meet somebody who knocks your socks off. And if you meet that person and you marry them, you're gonna be very happy being married. And if you don't meet that special person, you just stay happily single. Either way, you can't lose."

Ironically, as you all know, it's often when you finally accept being single and feel good about it that you meet someone. That is, when you're not really looking. But you have to *really* not be looking. You can't pretend that you're all happy and don't care, because it will show. Although, if you keep up the act long enough, you might actually start to believe it for a while. It's an old psychological trick.

It's hard when you're constantly being reminded of how incomplete you are if you're single. Whether it's your coupled friends, the obnoxious pair snuggling on the bus, your parents wondering if you'll "be bringing anyone to dinner with you," it's tough not to get down about being single once in a while.

"For a long time I felt guilty about being single," explains Yves. "There's a sense of shame around it, and I think a lot of gay men share that. That's why I think we're seeing this big push, in a way, for gay marriages right now. It's what I call 'The Tyranny of the Couple.' This idea that we're all supposed to be in these perfect little couples and unions.

"I met this really successful gay man in Toronto," he continues. "He's a physician – wealthy, bright, sweet and attractive. One Pride Day, we were getting ready to go out to the parade and he looked really depressed. I asked him what was wrong and he said, 'I still don't have a boyfriend. I feel like a failure as a gay man.' I think that's really cruel."

I agree with Yves. I think we need to put at least some of the energy we spend into trying to get everyone hitched into acknowledging that a lot of people are single, that people are single parents, that people are newly divorced and single, that people are over 30 and single, and that it's okay. That it doesn't mean you'll die pathetic and alone, surrounded by cats. Sure, it's not always easy or fun, but neither are relationships. And there's always TV.

"Mary Tyler Moore and Rhoda were really important for me in terms of identity," Yves explains. "I go from being either Mary or Rhoda. If I'm feeling depressed about being single and cracking one-liners about it, I'm Rhoda, but if I'm confident and happy about being a career girl, I'm Mary."

And you know what, Yves? We're gonna make it after all.

# The Science of Attraction
## A Lab Report

Attraction has always been a mystery. It's also highly subjective. What attracts one person may repulse another. It could be their smell, the way they walk, even their elbows.

As I said in the last chapter, the folks in the lab coats insist that much of what attracts us to each other is in our genes (not *those* jeans) and that our choice of dates is more biologically influenced than you might think. They've certainly done plenty of research to try and prove it. In fact, there's so much research being done on the science of attraction, I felt I should share some of it with you. Just so you know what you're up against. It'll also give you something to talk about on your next date.

As many of the people who spoke or wrote to me admitted in the last chapter, when it comes to attraction, beauty matters. In fact, our culture is pretty much obsessed with beauty. We use it to sell everything from cars to underwear. We cut ourselves up to maintain it. In fairy tales, the heroine is always beautiful, the villain uggers.

The media often gets blamed for this obsession. But, as some say, the media may only be reflecting what society wants. As Walter put it, "The media publishes images that reflect our desires. The media doesn't decide, 'We're gonna put a girl with a baboon head in this fashion magazine,' and then boom, if you put that image out there enough, people are suddenly gonna think girls with baboon heads are attractive." True enough, the media might not create the standard, but they do uphold it.

And standards of beauty do shift as a result of cultural and economic influences. At one time, larger women were considered more beautiful because it meant they were rich enough to eat. Consider also that Coco Chanel — the French designer who gave women the little black dress — was among the first people to think a suntan was sexy. Previously, women were supposed to keep their skin white, white, white to show they didn't have to work outdoors in the fields. But Chanel popularized the idea that a tan could result from an expensive vacation in the Tropics. (Of course, people didn't have to worry about the ozone layer in those days.)

Intelligence and personality can also influence our perception of beauty. And, as I mentioned earlier, someone can be beautiful until they open their mouth, and vice versa: a not so traditionally attractive person can be beautiful once you get to know them.

## A Question of Symmetry: Looking for the Perfect Mate

Beauty may well be in the eye of the beholder, but there is still a biological bottom line when it comes to what we find attractive — and according to the scientists, nothing can shake it. In fact, they've done studies with babies and found they look longer at what are considered typically "attractive" faces. And babies don't read fashion magazines.

Randy Thornhill, a professor of biology at the University of New Mexico, has done a lot of research into physical attraction. He says that, across backgrounds and cultures, when it comes to facial attraction, we all like the same fundamental things.

"If we set you or anybody else down and ask you to rate some pictures of people based on their attractiveness, your ratings would come out the same as anyone else's," he says. "You take pictures of Americans and you show them to Indians down in the jungles of Paraguay, and they react the same way as anyone else would. And you show Americans pictures of Paraguayan Indians and they'll react the same way."

The thing we are all most attracted to, according to Thornhill, is faces that are symmetrical, as in one side being an exact copy of the other. In order to prove this, scientists have done this neat thing, where they take a picture of a face and split it in half. They flip one side and place it so as to make a perfectly symmetrical image. If you're face is exactly symmetrical – and most faces aren't – the new face they've created will look the same as your actual face. But if the new face looks like if could be your evil twin, sorry, you're symmetrically challenged.

## Date from Hell

I was in Provincetown and I met this dyke who I ended up going for drinks with. I really liked her, and she said she wanted me to meet a friend of hers, so we went back to her motel room. Then in walked this other woman who looked exactly like me. So there I was sitting with my mirror image, and we both obviously wanted to sleep with this woman who'd invited us back to her room. I couldn't take it, so I finally left. Later that weekend she asked me back to her room again, but this time we were alone. I was definitely ready to get into bed with her, when she announced, "By the way, I forgot to tell you something. I'm married and I've never been with a woman before."

Symmetry – as in, one side of your face and body being a perfect replica of the other – is a very important criterion in our choice of mates, says Thornhill. The idea, from an evolutionary perspective, is that if you've got symmetry on your side, you'll survive better against the elements and thus be around longer for your kids. Imagine, for example, that a Tyrannosaurus Rex is after you and you have one leg that is a little longer than the other. Chances are you're not gonna get away as quickly and you might get squashed. So long, daddy.

"Symmetry shows how well the individual has done against the environmental and genetic challenges in the environment," explains Thornhill. "It's also a marker of developmental health. It indicates an absence of bad genes, which means that the symmetrical individual will have greater resistance to disease and defects."

His studies have shown that, in both animals and humans, those with the most symmetrical features have the most mates. And wouldn't you know it, turns out President Bill Clinton's face is perfectly symmetrical.

Apparently, according to Thornhill, symmetrical men even *smell* better to women. At least, according to a study in which they got men to wear T-shirts two nights in a row and then lined up women to smell them (where do I sign up?). Bingo, the more symmetrical men's T-shirts smelled better to the women. "Especially to women who were not on the pill and who were closest to mid-cycle. In other words, the most fertile women," he says.

Men like smelly women too. "According to our studies, men respond to women's scent most when the women are at their maximum fertility." (No, I'm sorry, I didn't ask how they figured that one out.) More on smells later…

Thornhill says that one of the other big factors when it comes to physical attractiveness is what he calls "hormone markers" – things like "muscles" on men or "breasts" on women. In other words, the lumps and bumps that let you know he's a he and she's a she.

"On a male body, for example, you'll see more muscles and more height. Those are features of testosterone," he explains. "On a female, you'll see a smaller waist, because of estrogen. We've studied the waist-hip ratio – the circumference of the waist divided by the circumference of the hips – in women and we've found that women with small waists and wider hips are considered more attractive." So *that's* why all the guys in the underwear ads are sportin' six packs, and short actors have to stand on boxes for their kissing scenes.

But what does this mean for all of us poor asymmetrical, hormonally challenged guys and girls? "We do the best we can," consoles Thornhill. "We see how attractive people are treated, even as children. Studies show that attractive kids make better grades and have more friends. And the same goes for adults.

"But we learn other social values as we grow up that make up for it. So if we're not as pretty as movie stars, we get more education and strive in other ways to try and compensate. And we bring all that to the mating game."

That's why beautiful people end up with beautiful people, Thornhill says. "Physically attractive people end up with physically attractive mates. They don't compromise on looks. They may compromise on intelligence or personality, but looks are very important to them."

So if you're beautiful, you'll probably end up with someone beautiful but stupid. Whereas ugly people end up with ugly people, but they have better personalities.

Sounds fair to me. Actually, before you hit the books or opt for facial surgery, I figure *most* people are moderately attractive and moderately intelligent, so we all stand a pretty good chance.

## Bucks and Beauty: Why Men Go After Looks and Women Go After Money

Okay, so what's with this stereotype that women go after money and men go after looks?

Studies of personal ads have backed this up, says Thornhill. They show that in these ads, men consistently describe what they're looking for in terms of physical appearance, whereas women look for personality and intelligence. We're too polite to come right out and ask for someone who's loaded, but focusing on intelligence and personality is apparently our way of saying we want someone who's smart and clever enough to be resourceful. That is, someone who can take care of both of you, plus any rug-rats you might produce together.

"It's the way we're designed," explains Thornhill. "Women were designed to look for good providers for their offspring, whereas men were designed just to want offspring."

The old spreading of the seed. But surely this must all be changing now that women are financially independent?

No way, says Thornhill. "You can't really change these things. We're genetically hard-wired."

Then how does this wiring reconcile itself with cultural changes? Such as the fact that women are making their own way in the world and not looking primarily to men for resources and financial security?

"It still doesn't change things, from what we've seen in the studies," says Thornhill. "Women with or without their own resources still want the guys with the status and resources."

In other words, no matter how filthy rich we women get, we still want a man who's at least as loaded as we are.

Douglas Kenrick, a professor of psychology at Arizona State University, backs this up. In his studies on age and mate selection, Kenrick looked at women with power and wealth, thinking that maybe they would stop looking for resources and start looking for hot young boy-toys. But they didn't, he says.

"They still looked for older men with resources," says Kenrick. "Even women with law and medical degrees were still looking for men who were more powerful and wealthy." So women who are wealthy and powerful give themselves even fewer men to choose from, while wealthy powerful men pretty much get their pick, since they'll settle for any pretty little thing who'll spend their money.

Kenrick and his colleagues also came up with some interesting results that support the "bucks and looks" theory. In one study, they showed various images to people and gauged their reactions.

"When we showed women an image of a powerful man, they felt less committed toward their own partners," Kenrick tells me. "And when men looked at an image of a beautiful woman, they became less committed to their partners." Again, women were attracted to power (i.e., money and resources), men to looks.

Kenrick and his team also looked at dominance and attraction, figuring that women who were more powerful and dominant would be more attractive to men. "Not the case," he says. "Men didn't care if she was powerful or wealthy, as long as she was beautiful."

Kenrick says that women have always been valued for their beauty and men for their power. "But how much of this is biological and how much is personal, historical and political is hard to determine."

According to Kenrick's study, seeing images of beautiful people in the media makes people rate average-looking people as less attractive. "We also looked at how our self-image is affected by what we see," he says. "Interestingly, we found that men were not affected by images of good-looking men but *were* affected by images of men who are go-getters and successful. An image of a 24-year-old guy running his own business led the men to lower their own estimation of how attractive or desirable they were."

As for women, he says, it didn't matter how dominant or successful the females in the images appeared. Rather, it was the images of beautiful women that caused us girls to lower our sense of desirability and attraction.

Hell, I don't need a university study to tell me that. It happens every time I flip through *Cosmo*. And you can't tell me *Cosmo* hasn't had some kind of influence.

## How Old Do You Think I Am?
## How Age Influences Our Date Selection

Age is another factor that both Thornhill and Kenrick cited as a big factor in determining attractiveness. Kenrick says that most research he came across had concluded that women are usually looking for men who are two to three years older, while men look for women who are two to three years younger. "This was described as the cultural norm for North America," he said.

But he suspected age difference had something to do with evolution. "We began by looking at personal ads all around the world, pretty much from every continent, including marital ads in India, and even data from Holland in the 1600s," says Kenrick.

Usually, in personal ads, people specify the age range that is acceptable to them in a potential partner. Example: "Hot young babe, 25, looking for rich man, aged 25-35."

What they found is that, on average, women were interested in guys their own age and up to nine or 10 years older. This preference didn't change, no matter how old the woman was.

"Basically, women, no matter how old they were, were less interested in younger men and would go for men up to nine years older," says Kenrick.

Conclusion: Women are looking for guys with resources, and those young whips don't usually have any. She wants an older fella who's established, but not so old that he'll die before she raises her children.

"Men, on the other hand, shifted their age preference as they got older," says Kenrick. "Men in their 20s were interested in women up to five years younger and up to five years older. Men in their 40s weren't interested in older women at all, but they were interested in women up to 15 years younger. And men in their 50s and 60s were ONLY interested in younger women – from five to six years younger and even up to 17 years younger."

Conclusion: Men are looking for fertility. Since men can pretty much father children until they croak, biologically speaking, women in their mid-20s are the most attractive to them because they are most fertile.

This pattern, Kenrick says, stayed consistent throughout the world and even throughout history. "A colleague had relatives on a tiny island in the Philippines," he says. "In this teeny little fishing village, the Catholic Church had marriage records dating back to 1913 that showed the same age-preference pattern in couples that we saw in other cultures."

Data from Holland from the 1600s also showed the same pattern. "And the more removed from North America and Europe you get, the more pronounced the pattern gets."

So, if I'm a 34-year-old woman, you're telling me I'm operating at an evolutionary disadvantage, and any guys with whom I do form a relationship will eventually leave me for a younger woman? Well, it seems this pattern is less pronounced in Western cultures.

Kenrick thinks this might be partly because women are aging more slowly and we're having children into their late 30s and early 40s without any problem. In other words, a woman at 40 is not as over-the-hill as a woman at that age once was. Whew, there's still hope, girls.

"As for older men leaving their partners for younger women, that may happen if a marriage breaks up or goes bad. But there is no underestimating the power of human bonding," Kenrick says. "If you've created and maintained a healthy bond with someone, it will stay strong. You don't question every day whether you should stay or not."

Besides, most of us don't consciously make our partnering decisions based on, "Oh, I'm looking for someone to reproduce with." And although men may be a little more blatant about the sexual nature of their quest, they're usually not thinking, "I want to spread my seed."

"It becomes a question of how much our intellect and social conditioning overrides our evolutionary and biological motivation," Kenrick says. "For example, we're programmed to become angry or annoyed in certain situations and even to want to kill someone, but most of us don't act on it."

So if we can't even use this information to excuse our irresponsible behavior, what's the point of knowing any of this? "The more we understand what drives our behavior, the better equipped we are to work with it," says Kenrick. "If we try to understand where the triggers are — in this case, the underlying biological motivation — maybe we can get a better understanding of ourselves."

Like why your husband just left you for a 21-year-old bimbo.

## Sex Smells: When It Comes to Sexual Attraction, Our Nose Knows

Even though we may finally admit that looks really are the first thing that attract us to someone, some research disputes this.

Jim Kohl is an American scientist based at the Partell Medical Center in Las Vegas. He's been studying the relationship between sex and smells for more than 10 years. Kohl and his colleague, Robert T. Francoeur, have published their research in a book called *The Scent of Eros: Mysteries of Odor in Human Sexuality* (1995). According to Kohl, you could like everything about someone, but if you don't like the way they smell, forget it. Especially if he or she smells like someone you've turned your nose up at in the past.

"In reality," Kohl told me over the phone from his office at the center, "we make the odor association first and the visual association afterwards."

And while we're on the subject of smells and human sexuality, we can turn to our four-legged friends for some insight. In his book, *A Natural History of Sex* (1993), Adrian Forsyth describes how mammals rely heavily on smell and taste to check out each other's sexual status. Get this: billy goats spray urine – and even ejaculate – into their own beards to let the lady goats know they're randy.

Testing humans in this area is tricky, obviously. But Kohl says a few studies have been done to suggest that men find women's vaginal odors more pleasant around the time of ovulation, when they are most fertile.

How does someone's smell trigger attraction? The connection is subliminal and has to do with something called pheromones: chemicals in our sweat that trigger hormones in our brain. It seems there literally is chemistry between two people who find themselves attracted to each other.

The theory goes that when you're hanging out with other people, say in a crowded bar, pheromones are flying all over the place. If I connect with the smell of your pheromones and you connect with the smell of my pheromones, that spark may result.

So all the energy we put into meeting the right person is pretty much futile, because it all comes down to, "I don't like the way you smell"?

"We are animals," says Kohl, "and we do share some animal responses. But how much our intellect overrides our natural odor associations remains to be determined."

Kohl and Francoeur agree that a big part of the smell response goes back to memory and learned associations. Kohl calls this "olfactory imprinting" and likens it to visual imprinting for ducks. (If the first thing a baby duck sees is its mother, it will follow her around. If it sees a basketball, it'll follow that. Same with olfactory imprinting.) So if someone smells like your favorite blanky when you were a kid, you may start following him or her around, because they remind you of the warmth and security of your childhood.

Before you head out to the bar and start sniffing the guy on the next barstool, remember what Kohl said. Yes, we are animals, but we do have an intellect that often overrides our animal instincts. What attracts one person to another may be complex from a scientific point of view, but ultimately we all know it when we feel it. How we act on it is what's important. And when you're contemplating action is when you don't necessarily want to rely on your animal instincts. The other people in the bar might not appreciate you peeing in your own beard.

## Queer Query

Of course, all this research is based on the idea that we need to be attracted to each other in order to keep the species going, to reproduce. So how do you explain gay attraction?

"The scientific studies show that the only thing that differs between the homosexual and heterosexual is the sex of the preferred sex object," Thornhill says. (I wouldn't say it's exactly the *only* thing, but you know what he means.) "So homosexual men like men, heterosexual men like women. If you look at their sexuality, it's the same in the sense that both heterosexual and homosexual men are both very into casual sex if they can get it. They're both into sexual variety."

In other words, both gay and straight guys will fuck anything that moves. So just because gays are attracted to other men, it doesn't change their reproductive instincts? They still want to spread their seed?

"Right," says Thornhill. "Also, homosexual men are just as into looks as heterosexual men. Now a heterosexual man who's not very good looking still could attract a woman if he's got status and resources. But if men have to attract other men, they have to make themselves look good because guys are into looks when it comes to seeking out a mate, whether that mate is male or female."

Which explains why gay men dress so much better.

In his study of age preference in personal ads, Kenrick also found that homosexual men have the same pattern as heterosexual men. "Gay men in their 20s advertised for guys from five years older to five years younger than them," Kenrick tells me. "As they got older, they asked for progressively younger and younger men. So that gay men in their 50s were looking for partners from five years younger to 20 years younger than themselves.

"As for lesbians, again, the pattern was similar to that of heterosexual women," he adds. "Lesbian women in their 50s were interested in women two years older down to about seven years younger."

For Kenrick, this data only reinforces the biological nature behind attraction. Gay men want younger guys, just like straight guys want younger, theoretically more fertile, women. "A gay man is looking for a young attractive partner with whom to reproduce, even though he's not going to reproduce with another man," he says.

"You would think homosexual men could say, 'I'm not playing the reproduction game and instead I'll find a guy my age, one I can relate to and talk to.' They should be freed of this biological motivation behind mate selection, but our studies show they aren't."

Which means if you're a, uh, *mature* gay man, you really lose out. Because like your straight counterparts, if you haven't already got a partner, you're gonna want to go after the younger boys. But whereas the straight old guys can usually find younger women who will be attracted to them, especially if they're filthy rich, young gay men are gonna be less interested in older men, in the same way that straight boys are less interested in older women.

But wait. Before all you mature gay men and heterosexual women of a certain age throw in the towel, remember there's a lot more to attraction than science. And trust me, even in the human jungle, there are plenty of exceptions to the rules. I've certainly seen a few young gay men who had no problem dating filthy-rich older men, and I've seen a woman in her 40s whooping it up with a guy half her age.

So rev up your intellect, throw on your sexiest outfit, turn on your most dazzling smile and get out there.

# 12

# You're Gonna
# Make It After All

## Final Words

There you have it. A view from the dating frontlines – from the experts, the lab coats and the single people in the trenches.

Yes, it's a tough battle sometimes. Sometimes you get hurt and sometimes it's tempting to just throw in the towel and go M.I.A.

But every so often, you taste victory – "He called me back!" or "She likes collecting doorknobs too!" – and it makes you want to press on.

Dating can be discouraging and confusing, but it can also be exciting. We wouldn't really want it any other way, would we?

The one heartening thing is that you do get better at it with experience. And the only way to get experience is to practise. As we've told you several times now, Mr. or Ms. Right isn't going to fall from the sky.

But the beauty of it is that, eventually, if you do it really well, you'll never have to do it again. Because you'll have found someone who will be there to feed the pigeons with you when the eyesight starts to go.

Now go forth and date!

Yup, that's it for now. But we'd love to hear from you. Drop us a line with some of your dating tips and horror stories, and who knows, maybe they'll turn up in Josey's next book (anonymously, of course)! Just write to:

Dating
c/o Adams Media Corporation
260 Center Street
Holbrook, MA 02343